Pure design
Objects of desire

Pure design
Objects of desire

monsa

Pure design

Is there more to this than just pure design? On the one hand we have shapes, colours and textures and on the other, the hidden story, a symbol, a concept, pure creativity erases the already blurred division between art and industrial design. Pure design proposes a cocktail of sensations: Purely beautiful objects, a delight on the eyes, pleasant vibes and refined ambiences, hidden meanings, reminiscences, pure untainted emotions. We propose a journey through a meticulous assortment of projects filled with emotion. The combination of this emotional and visual experience transforms some of our everyday objects into veritable works of art. The formal and semantic, at times, almost poetic language, dressed as it is with a touch of humour or irony tells us a story and transports us to the most intimate world of each of the "pure designers". This book hopes to reveal a different side to industrial design. Since this creative discipline first began, modern techniques, trends, practical virtues and technological advancements have all contributed towards a great evolutionary process which in turn has brought great diversification. Not confined to improving practical and aesthetic qualities but also creating new objects and inventing new uses, relating stories, remembering the past, stirring emotions, explore new fields…

From cover to cover, this book fully expounds the double meaning of PURE and acquaints the reader with some of those "pure designers", amongst which some have already made their mark whilst others are about to do so.

¿Puro diseño o diseño puro? Por un lado tenemos formas, colores, materiales, por otro lado, una historia escondida, un símbolo, un concepto, una pura originalidad que difumina más aún, la borrosa línea que separa el arte del diseño industrial. Pure design nos propone un cóctel de sensaciones: Objetos puramente bellos, sensaciones suaves y refinadas, un placer para la vista, unos significados escondidos, algunos recuerdos, puras emociones. Nos invita a un recorrido a través de una minuciosa selección de proyectos llenos de sensibilidad. Un viaje emocional y visual. La mezcla de estos dos factores hace de algunos de los objetos de nuestra vida diarias, verdaderas obras de arte. El lenguaje formal y semántico, a veces poético y aliñado con un toque de humor o ironía, nos cuenta una historia y nos lleva al mundo íntimo y personal de cada uno de los "pure designers". Este libro nos revela otra cara del diseño industrial. La técnica, las modas, la funcionalidad, los avances tecnológicos, han hecho que esta disciplina creativa evolucionara mucho desde su creación, y que su función se diversifique. No solo se trata de mejorar la funcionalidad y la estética, también se pueden crear nuevos objetos, nuevas funciones, contar historias, recordar el pasado, emocionar, explorar nuevos campos…

A lo largo de este libro podréis entender el doble sentido de PURE y descubrir algunos de los "pure designers". Entre ellos algunos ya han marcado pautas en el mundo del diseño y otros lo harán muy pronto.

Bon voyage!

Julien Martinez Calmettes

PURE DESIGN
Copyright © 2006 Instituto Monsa de ediciones, S.A

Author / Autor
Textos, diseño y maquetación
Text, design and layout:
Julien Martinez Calmettes
Equipo editorial Monsa

Editor
Josep María Minguet

Art director / Director de Arte
Louis Bou

Translation / Traducción
Babyl traducciones

© INSTITUTO MONSA DE EDICIONES, S.A
Gravina 43 (08930)
Sant Adrià de Besòs
Barcelona
Tlf. +34 93 381 00 50
Fax.+34 93 381 00 93
www.monsa.com
monsa@monsa.com

ISBN: 84-96429-31-8
D.L: B-7093-2006

Printed by / Impreso por
Industrias Gráficas Mármol, S.L

In this page / en esta página
PATERE
Big Game
Photo / Foto: Milo Keller
In collaboration with Adrien Rovero.
Colaboración con Adrien Rovero.
www.adrienrovero.com

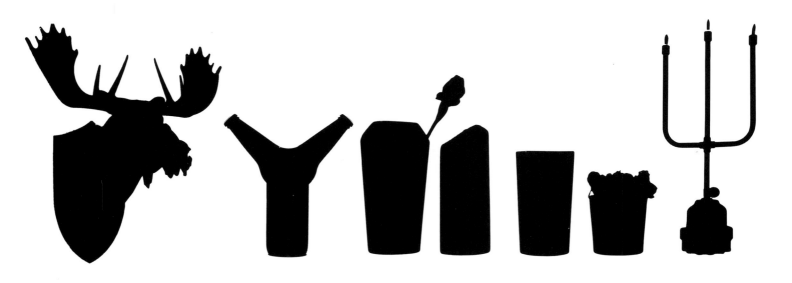

Pure objects

The table is set

HANDLE PLATE
Meric Kara@Fabrica

"A connection between the kitchen and the table."
This ceramic plate has a plastic pan type handle, symbolizing
the link between the kitchen and the table.

Plato de cerámica con mango de plástico, simbolizando la
conexión entre la cocina y la mesa.

WEGE, frying pan 2005
Mikko Laakkonen@Rehti
Photo: Timo Ryttäri

With this frying pan, meat can be adorned with vegetable
motifs, transformed into a culinary graphic support.
Materials: cast iron and wood.
Dimensions: ø 27cm
Made by Selki-Asema.

Gracias a esta sartén se puede estampar un motivo vegetal en
un trozo de carne, convirtiéndolo en soporte gráfico culinario.
Materiales: hierro de fundición y madera.
Dimensiones: ø 27cm
Fabricado por Selki-Asema.

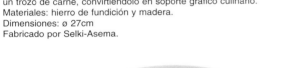

COFFEE DROP SPLASH, BISCUIT 1994
Radi designers
Foto : Patrick Gries
Designed to adapt to any coffee cup, this biscuit symbolizes a spattered coffee and illustrates the ritual: "Never a coffee without chocolate".
Dimensions: H 2.7 x Ø 8 cm
Materials: chocolate covered biscuit.

Diseñada para adaptarse a cualquier taza de café, esta galleta simboliza una salpicadura de café e ilustra la costumbre: "Nunca un café sin chocolate".
Dimensiones: H 2.7 x Ø 8 cm
Materiales: galleta bañada en chocolate.

CHOW BELLA
Joe Doucet@Intotonyc
Hopsticks and holder.
Chopsticks and holder
This piece of fine porcelain allows the chopsticks
to be presented side by side and protects the
tablecloth at the same time.
Materials: wood and porcelain.
Chopstick: 25cm
Holder: 1.5cm x 4cm ø 2cm

Palillos y su soporte.
Esta fina pieza de porcelana permite presentar
juntos los dos palillos y sirve a la vez de salva
mantel.
Materiales: madera y porcelana.
Palillo: 25cm
Soporte: 1,5cm x 4cm ø 2cm

SUPPA, table cloth 2005
Mikko laakkonen@Rehti
Table cloth which serves as a fruit bowl.
Material: wool felt.
Prototype.

Mantel de mesa con finalidad de frutero.
Materiales: wool felt.
Prototipo.

SUGAR SPOON
Meric Kara@Fabrica
Never again will our tea or coffee be over sugared!
This spoon is designed to measure exactly the
required amount of sugar.

¡Se acabó el café o el té demasiado dulce! Esta
cuchara permite dosificar la cantidad exacta de un
terrón de azúcar.

GUGGENHEIM SUGAR 2004
Toshihiko Sakai@Sakai Design Associate
Guggenheim Museum Exhibition Museum Goods 2004
Sugar lumps specially made for the Guggenheim museum.

Terrón de azúcar realizado para el museo Gugenheim.

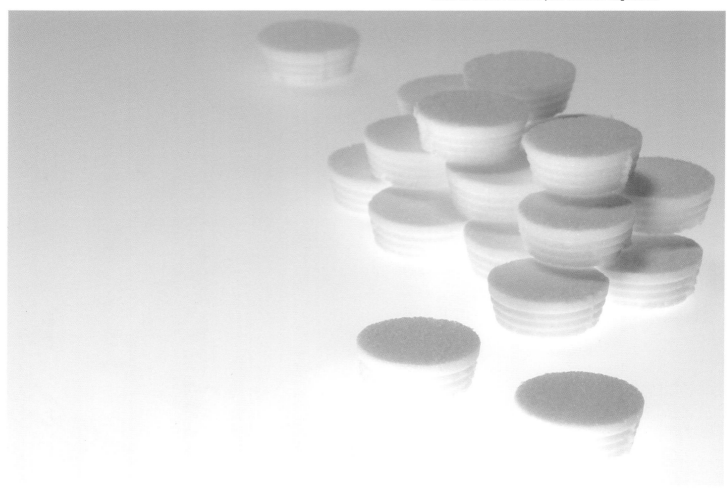

SLICE BOWL
SLICE PLATS
SLICE TASSE
Sam Barron
A set of designer ceramic crockery.
Coffee cups, plates, dishes.
Material: ceramic.

Serie de creaciones de cerámica.
Taza de café, platos.
Material: cerámica.

PARENTHESE
Ricardo Bustos
"Parenthesis" tray.
Material: ceramic.

Bandeja "Paréntesis".
Material: cerámica.

LA PREMIERE BOUCHEE
THE FIRST BIT
Mathieu Lehanneur
Photo: Véronique Huygues
Those undergoing medical treatment will be able
to take their daily oral dose as simple as eating
their daily meal, thanks to this pill which attaches
to a fork making the patient's first mouthful a
therapeutic one. Since medication is to be taken
habitually and rigidly, this method guarantees its
constant presence, forming part of the most
basic daily routines such as laying the table.

Las personas sometidas a tratamiento médico,
podrían hacer de la toma diaria por vía oral, algo
tan normal como comer, gracias a una pastilla
que se acopla al tenedor haciendo del primer
bocado del paciente un bocado terapéutico. El
medicamento no se debe olvidar, pero de esta
forma está presente, se adapta a los ritmos de
vida y se integra a los gestos cotidianos más
sencillos como poner la mesa.

TORIQUE COLLECTION 1999
Ronan and Erwan Bouroullec
Photo: Morgane Le Gall
Vase, stool, jug, table, oil lamp, fruit
bowl.
These pieces are from a collection of
objects created as part of a joint project
in 1999 with potter, Claude Aiello.

Florero, taburete, jarro, mesa, lámpara
de aceite , frutero.
Estas piezas de cerámica forman parte
de una colección de objetos creados
en 1999 en colaboración con el
ceramista Claude Aiello.

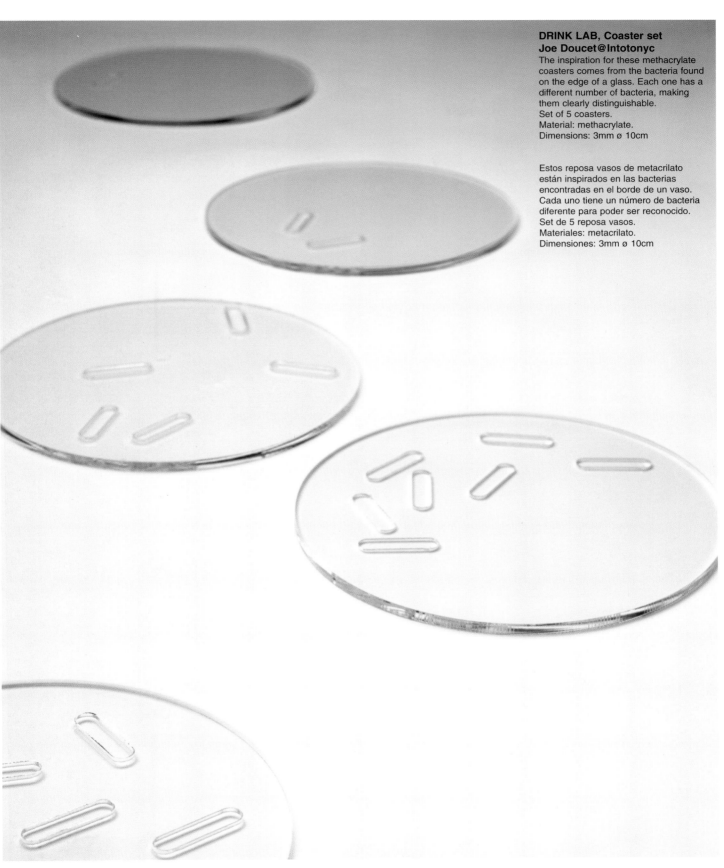

DRINK LAB, Coaster set
Joe Doucet@Intotonyc
The inspiration for these methacrylate coasters comes from the bacteria found on the edge of a glass. Each one has a different number of bacteria, making them clearly distinguishable.
Set of 5 coasters.
Material: methacrylate.
Dimensions: 3mm ø 10cm

Estos reposa vasos de metacrilato están inspirados en las bacterias encontradas en el borde de un vaso. Cada uno tiene un número de bacteria diferente para poder ser reconocido.
Set de 5 reposa vasos.
Materiales: metacrilato.
Dimensiones: 3mm ø 10cm

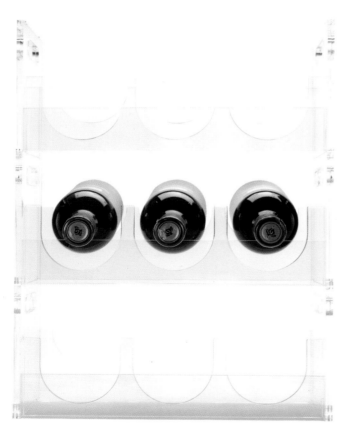

BOTELLERO
Muji

Transparent methacrylate wine rack. Individual units can be combined and stacked as required. The material used in manufacture makes the wine rack almost invisible, leaving the apparently levitating bottles of wine as the central feature. Material: Methacrylate.

Botellero transparente de metacrilato. Apilando y juntando los elementos se puede crear un botellero a medida según las necesidades. El material utilizado hace que el botellero sea casi invisible y deje el protagonismo a unas botellas de vino que parecen levitar.
Material: Metacrilato.

WINE CRADLE
Suck UK

This extremely simple piece fixed to the wall supports the indispensable "kit" for a romantic dinner or aperitif.
Material: stainless steel.

Esta sencillísima pieza fijada en una pared, soporta el "kit" indispensable para una cena o un aperitivo romántico.
Materiales: acero inoxidable.

PILE WINE RACK
Harry Allen

"REALITY" is a collection of objects which emulate the reality.
More than just an original design, Harry Allen sought to emulate the inherent beauty of the surrounding objects.
Materials: polyester resin, moulded silicon.

"REALITY" es una serie de objetos cuyas formas copian la realidad. Mas que originalidad en las formas, Harry Allen busca la belleza inherente de las cosas que le rodean.
Materiales: resina de poliéster, molde de silicona.

WINEGLASS
Meric Kara@Fabrica
For drinking straight from
the bottle.

Para beber directamente
de la botella.

CHEESE PLATE 2003-2005
Meric Kara@Fabrica
An original cheese board complete with a
trap, but this time for humans.

Una original bandeja de quesos, con
trampa, pero esta vez para humanos.

DROP
Joe Doucet@Intotonyc

Drop is a set of glasses inspired by the first "high speed" photographs taken by Harold Edgerton which immortalised the impact of milk drops, and revealed the hidden world around us. Each glass is traditionally crafted by an expert glass blower, making each one unique.
Material: blown glass.
Dimensions:
Large: 15cm ø 6,4cm
Small: 6,4cm ø 6,4cm

Drop es un set de vasos inspirados en las primeras fotos "high speed" realizadas por Harold Edgerton que inmortalizaban los impactos de gotas de leche, revelándonos el mundo escondido que nos rodea. Cada vaso esta realizado por un maestro vidriero de forma artesanal, convirtiendo cada uno de ellos en objetos únicos.
Materiales: vidrio soplado.
Dimensiones:
Grande: 15cm ø 6,4cm
Pequeño: 6,4cm ø 6,4cm

BOTTLE OPENER 2005
Suck Uk
An ingenious and practical
bottle opener which sticks to
the fridge thanks to its
magnetic surface.

Un ingenioso y práctico
abridor que se pega a la
nevera gracias a su superficie magnetizada.

"Vipp et les trente artistes" 2005
Cédric Ragot
A Vipp rubbish bin customised for a
"Handicap International" charity auction.

Customización de un cubo de basura Vipp
para una subasta benéfica de "Handicap
International".

RANDOM 2003
Meric Kara@Fabrica
Surprise can. Fanta? Sprite?
Coca cola? Juice?
Seen at the "Inside design
Amsterdam" 2003.

Lata sorpresa. ¿Fanta?
¿Sprite? ¿Coca cola? ¿Zumo?
Expuesto en "Inside design
Amsterdam" 2003.

SHARE 2003-2005
Meric Kara@Fabrica
Sharing your beer is now
possible thanks to this
mutated bottle.

Compartir su cerveza es
ahora posible gracias a
esta botella mutante.

KULT breakfast range 2000-2005
Sebastian Bergne
An original collection to use at breakfast time.
Materials: ceramic, stainless steel and glass.
Made by WMF.

Gama de productos originales para el desayuno.
Materiales: cerámica, acero inoxidable y vidrio.
Fabricado por WMF.

BOP place setting 2003
Sebastian Bergne

A place setting including plates, a glass
and a tray. Each item in the set can be
positioned exactly according to the fine
lines shown in relief on the tray.
Materials: ABS, ceramic.
Made by Driade, D-house.

Set compuesto de platos, vaso y bandeja.
La bandeja ubica gracias a unas finas
líneas en relieve, la posición exacta de
cada elemento que compone el set.
Materiales: ABS, cerámica.
Fabricado por Driade, D-house.

STAK Table set 2003
Karim Rashid
Two tone stackable crockery set.
Produced by Danese Milano.
Material: ceramic.

Set de piezas bicolores apilables.
Producido por Danese Milano.
Material: cerámica.

Play

PANIER PERCE
Iona Vautrin & Guillaume Delvigne

A few threads of wool and a little imagination are all that's needed to add a personal touch this white ceramic basket. On a technical level, all you need is a grandmother prepared to teach you the legendary art of cross stitch.
Materials: ceramic and wool.

Unos hilos de lana de color y un poco de imaginación son los ingredientes que se necesitan para personalizar esta pequeña cesta de cerámica blanca. A nivel técnico, solo necesitáis una abuela dispuesta a enseñaros el legendario punto de cruz.
Materiales: cerámica y lana.

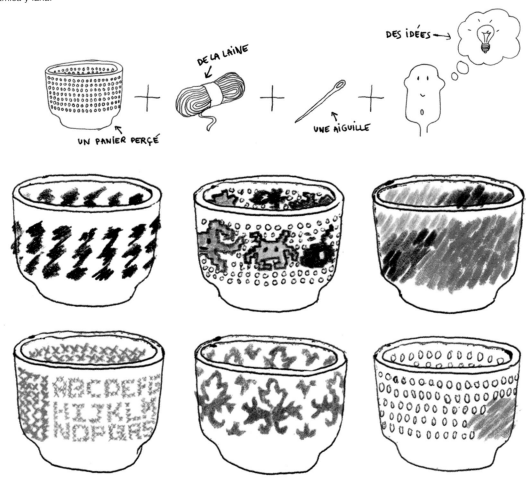

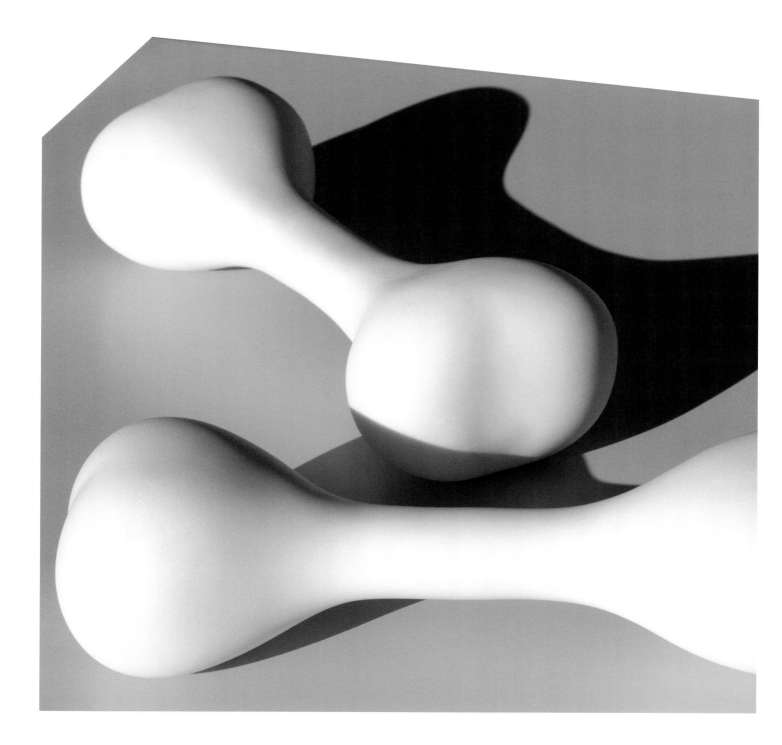

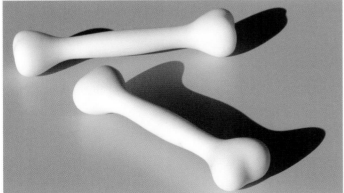

FOREVERYOUNG 2004
Robert Stadler
Photo : Patrick Gries
Dumbbells made in Pietrasanta (Italy) in white marble from Carrara.
Limited edition of 12 dumbbells 3.5kg and 1.2.kg
Galerie Dominique Fiat, Paris.

Mancuernas realizadas en Pietrasanta (Italia) en mármol blanco de Carrara.
Edición limitada de 12 unidades de 3,5 kg y 1,2kg
Galerie Dominique Fiat, París.

LE CROCODILE ÉCHAPPE À NOTRE GOURMANDISE EN SE RÉFUGIANT DANS SA CAGE.

ALCATRAZ
Iona Vautrin & Guillaume Delvigne

Resisting temptation will be easier thanks to this jail in which those famous crocodile shaped sweets remain duly protected.
Material: ceramic.

Resistir a la gula será más fácil gracias a esta jaula donde se refugian los famosos caramelos en forma de cocodrilo.
Material: cerámica.

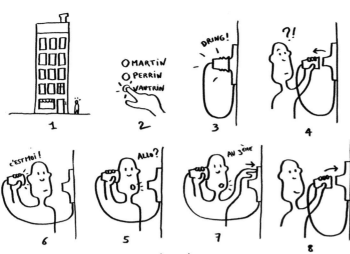

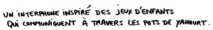

UN INTERPHONE INSPIRÉ DES JEUX D'ENFANTS
QUI COMMUNIQUENT À TRAVERS LES POTS DE YAHOURT.

ALLO?!
Iona Vautrin & Guillaume Delvigne
An entry phone full of greetings and inspired by the childhood game using two tins connected by string.
Material: ceramic.

Un portero eléctrico lleno de recuerdos, inspirado en el juego infantil de las latas comunicadas por un hilo.
Material: cerámica.

FOOT BOWL 2004
Nahoko Koyama and Alex Garnett@Mixko

There appears at times to be no relation between form and function. In this case a slight deformation creates a new role, a fruit bowl from a football. A slight adjustment also to the name gives a whole new meaning.

Dimensions: ø 75cm
Material: Ceramic.

La forma y la función a veces no coinciden mucho. En este caso una ligera deformación lleva a una nueva función. Como conseguir un frutero con una pelota de football. El nombre también se modifica un poco y cambia el sentido.

Dimensiones: ø 75cm
Material: Cerámica.

SCREW-HEAD ASHTRAY 2003
Nahoko Koyama & Alex Garnett@Mixko
What happens when we increase the size of a very small object?
In this case, the head of a crosshead screw becomes an original
ashtray. Size is a dominating factor, something well understood by
these two young designers whose creations are often based on
scale adjustments.
Dimensions: 4.5cm x 15.5cm ø 15.5cm
Material: ceramic with a metallic finish.

¿Qué pasa si aumentamos la talla de un objeto muy pequeño?
Una cabeza de tornillo estrella se podría convertir en un original
cenicero. El tamaño si que importa en este caso y estos dos
jóvenes diseñadores lo han comprendido perfectamente y sus
creaciones juegan mucho con los cambios de escala.
Dimensiones: 4,5cm x 15,5cm ø 15,5cm
Material: cerámica metalizada.

DO BREAK 2001
Janneke Hooymans & Frank
Tjepkema@Tjep
In collaboration with Peter van der Jagt
Photo: Bianca Pilet
To break or not to break? That is the
question. With this flower vase we have a
choice of the two options. It can be hurled
to the floor creating a beautiful, unique
and personalised object, which still
remains intact and watertight, thanks to
the layer of silicon on the inside. The very
thing to overcome a fit of temper.

Materials: Porcelain and silicon.
Dimensions: 34cm
Produced by Droog Design for Do.

¿Romper o no romper? Esa es la
cuestión. Este florero permite las dos
opciones. Tirándolo al suelo obtenemos
un objeto personalizado bello y único.
Gracias a una capa de silicona en su
interior, los trozos se quedan bien en su
sitio y la impermeabilidad se conserva.
Un objeto perfecto para superar sus
nervios.

Materiales: Porcelana y silicona,
Dimensiones: 34cm
Producido por Droog Design for Do.

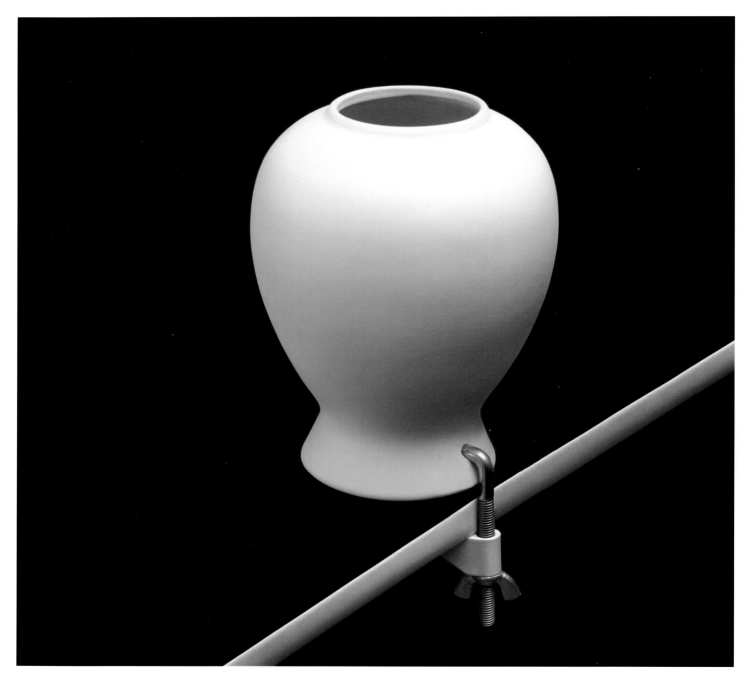

FIXED VASE 2003-2005
Meric Kara@Fabrica
To break or not to break? In this case, not to break. This
device secures the vase to the table preventing any
such event. An ideal gift for clumsy people.
Material: ceramic, steel.

¿Romper o no romper? En este caso, no romper. El
sistema de fijación a la mesa puede evitar un disgusto.
Un regalo perfecto para la gente torpe.
Material: cerámica, acero.

DIGITAL CANDLE 2003-2005
Meric Kara@Fabrica
With 40 candles and this specially designed base
any number can be written up to 99.
Exhibited at the "Milan furniture Fair 2005"
Produced by Paola C.

Utilizando 40 velas podéis escribir en este soporte
cualquier numero hasta 99.
Expuesto en el "Milan furniture Fair 2005"
Producido por Paola C.

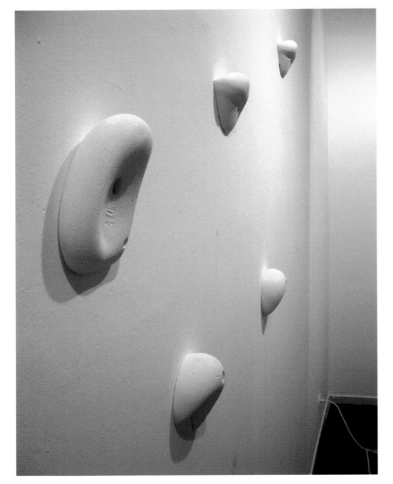

YOSEMITE Coat rack.
Cul de Sac

This design is in response to the atypical use of objects
in an exercise which is totally out of context. In this case
the artificial climbing wall attachments, where people
normally hang, are used to create an original coat rack.

Esta propuesta responde al uso atípico de un objeto en
un ejercicio de descontextualización. Así, las presas de
escalada de las que se cuelgan algunas personas se
convierten en un original perchero.

SALERO TO-KIO
Cul de Sac
A moving saltcellar inspired by clockwork toys.
Passing the salt to a fellow diner becomes a
form of play.

Un salero móvil inspirado en los juguetes de
cuerda. Pasar la sal a su vecino de mesa se
convierte en un juego.

battleships napkin ©thrink

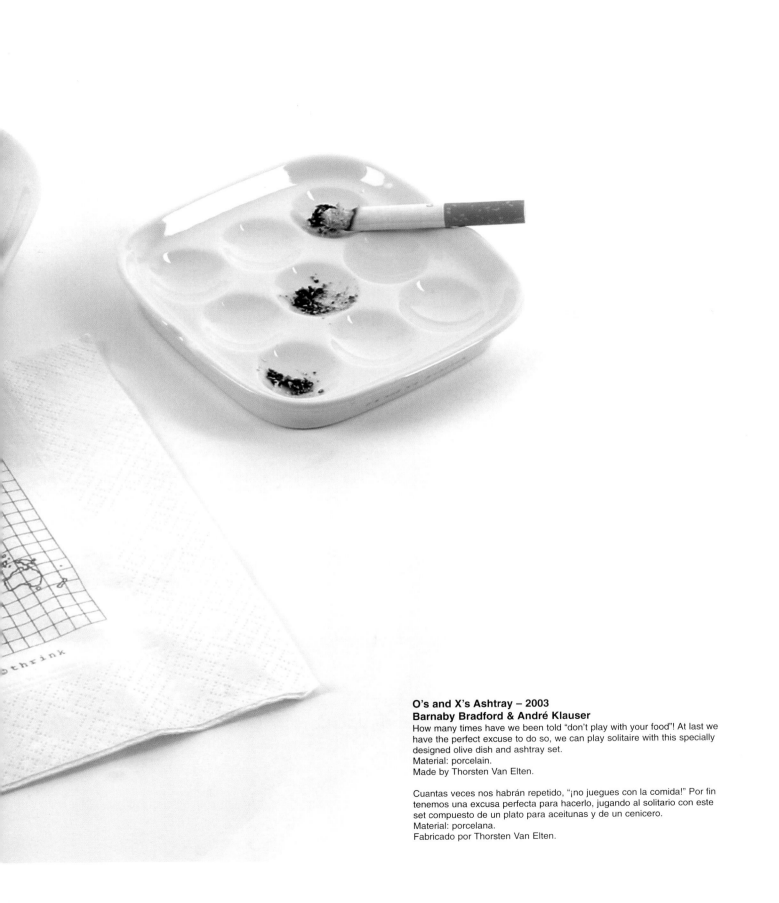

O's and X's Ashtray – 2003
Barnaby Bradford & André Klauser
How many times have we been told "don't play with your food"! At last we
have the perfect excuse to do so, we can play solitaire with this specially
designed olive dish and ashtray set.
Material: porcelain.
Made by Thorsten Van Elten.

Cuantas veces nos habrán repetido, "¡no juegues con la comida!" Por fin
tenemos una excusa perfecta para hacerlo, jugando al solitario con este
set compuesto de un plato para aceitunas y de un cenicero.
Material: porcelana.
Fabricado por Thorsten Van Elten.

RAT WALLPAPER
Front design
Photo: Ana Lönnerstam.
A roll of white wallpaper is eaten by a mouse which
becomes a designer for the day. The holes create an
original and uniquely repetitive pattern through which the
old wallpaper can be seen.

Un rollo de papel de pared blanco comido por una ratita
convertida en diseñadora por un día. Los agujeros crean
un motivo repetido, original y único dejando ver por
zonas el antiguo papel.

STAMPCUPS 2004
Valeria Miglioli & Barnaby Barford
It is now possible to transform those typical and rather
irritating coffee cup stains into a beautiful flower motif.
Never before have these stains been so much appreci-
ated and so decorative. Each cup displays a pattern in
relief on the base.
Set of two cups.
Material: Porcelain.
Made by Thorsten Van Elten.

Convertir las típicas e irritantes manchas de café que
forman las tazas en un precioso motivo floral es ahora
posible. Las manchas nunca han sido tan bienvenidas
y decorativas. El relieve de la base de cada taza actúa
como un tampón de imprenta.
Set de dos Tazas.
Material: Porcelana.
Fabricado por Thorsten Van Elten.

PUBLIC CLOCK 2004
Nicolas Le Moigne
This clock is based on the same system used for train station information boards,
the hour written as if it were the answer to the question "What time is it?", "it is a
quarter past two". The board can also be used to write any message, such as
"Happy Christmas".
Material: aluminium.
Dimensions: 400cm x 30cm x 30cm
Made by Omega Electronics.
First prize winner in a competition to design a public clock for the city of Geneva.
Locality: Place Neuve, Geneva, Switzerland.

Este reloj utiliza el sistema usado por los paneles de las estaciones de tren, con
la particularidad de escribir la hora con palabras como si fuera la respuesta a la
pregunta "¿Que hora es?, "son las dos y cuarto". Permite también escribir
cualquier mensaje como por ejemplo "feliz navidad".
Material: aluminio
Dimensiones: 400cm x 30cm x 30cm
Fabricado por Omega Electronics.
Ganó el primer premio del concurso para la creación de un reloj público para la
cuidad de Ginebra.
Localización: Place Neuve, Ginebra, Suiza.

re vingt-cinq

E-MONEY
Suck UK
A moneybox inspired by a computer keyboard and treated with growth hormone. For those who still prefer to save money at home.

Una hucha directamente sacada del teclado de un ordenador y criada con hormona de crecimiento. Para los que siguen ahorrando dinero en casa.

Old story

SANTA MARÍA
Cul de sac

To analysis and isolate an object firmly instilled in most minds as beautiful and evocative and to recreate that object in this new material (papier-mâché), to create a modern object of desire with profound psychological undertones. Created by means of a basically simple manufacturing process, in this case papier-mâché on a Santa María cast mould, combining traditional craftsmanship and modern design, character and concept. Made by Cul de Sac in a joint project with craftswoman Verónica Palomares.

Analizar y aislar un objeto incrustado en la memoria de la mayoría de las personas, sugerente y evocador, y reeditarlo en este nuevo material (Cartón Piedra), para conseguir una pieza actual, pero con una carga psicológica muy importante, capaz de convertirlo en objeto de deseo. Mediante un proceso de elaboración en principio sencillo como es el cartón piedra sobre molde de escayola Santa María se convierte en un proyecto que mezcla artesanía y diseño, alma y concepto. Realizado por Cul de Sac en colaboración con la artesana Verónica Palomares.

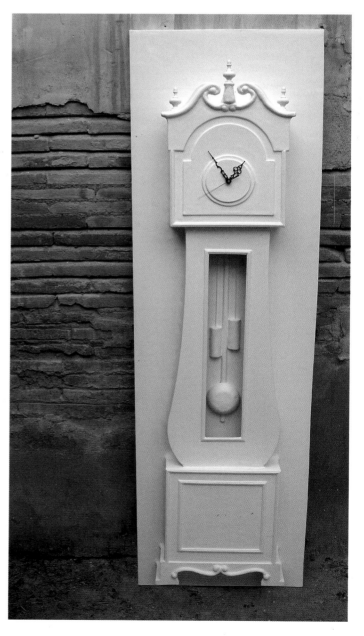

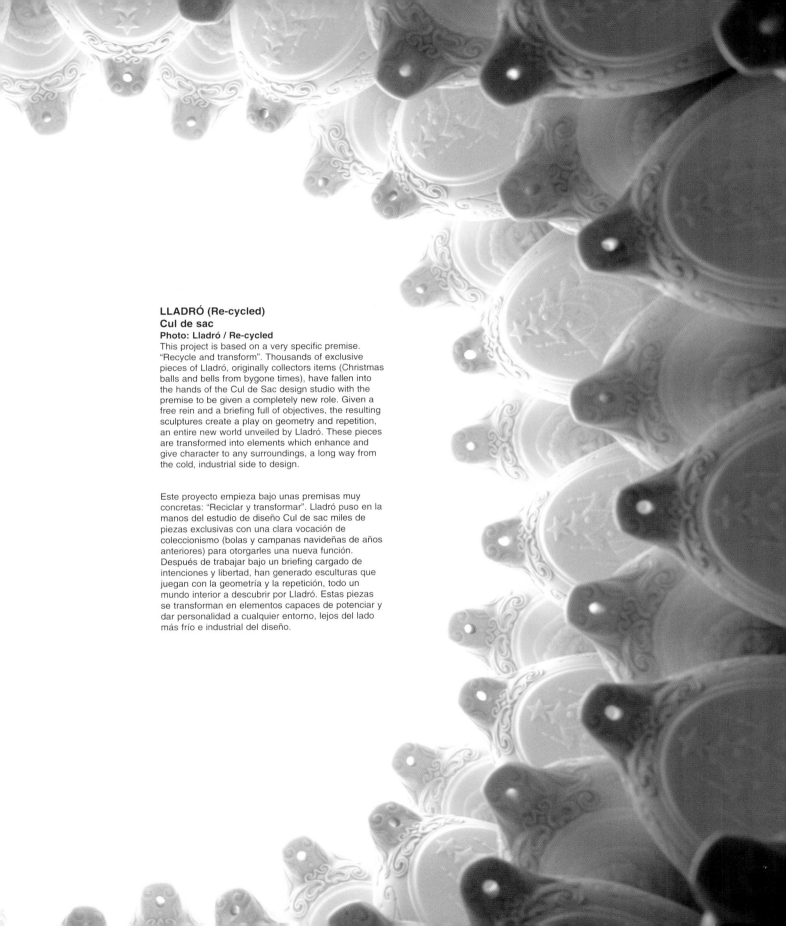

LLADRÓ (Re-cycled)
Cul de sac
Photo: Lladró / Re-cycled

This project is based on a very specific premise. "Recycle and transform". Thousands of exclusive pieces of Lladró, originally collectors items (Christmas balls and bells from bygone times), have fallen into the hands of the Cul de Sac design studio with the premise to be given a completely new role. Given a free rein and a briefing full of objectives, the resulting sculptures create a play on geometry and repetition, an entire new world unveiled by Lladró. These pieces are transformed into elements which enhance and give character to any surroundings, a long way from the cold, industrial side to design.

Este proyecto empieza bajo unas premisas muy concretas: "Reciclar y transformar". Lladró puso en la manos del estudio de diseño Cul de sac miles de piezas exclusivas con una clara vocación de coleccionismo (bolas y campanas navideñas de años anteriores) para otorgarles una nueva función. Después de trabajar bajo un briefing cargado de intenciones y libertad, han generado esculturas que juegan con la geometría y la repetición, todo un mundo interior a descubrir por Lladró. Estas piezas se transforman en elementos capaces de potenciar y dar personalidad a cualquier entorno, lejos del lado más frío e industrial del diseño.

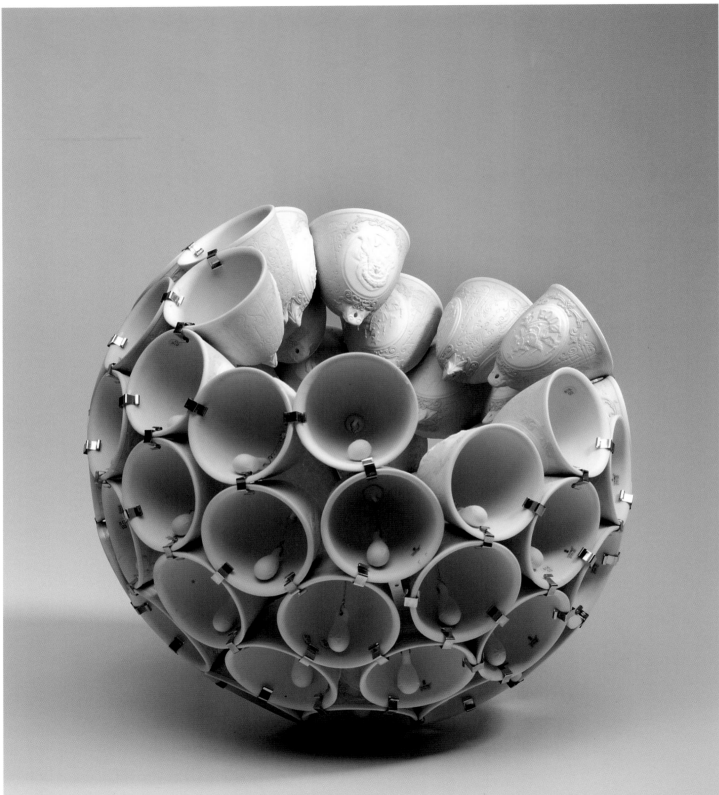

LLADRÓ (Re-cycled)
Cul de sac
Photo: Lladró / Re-cycled

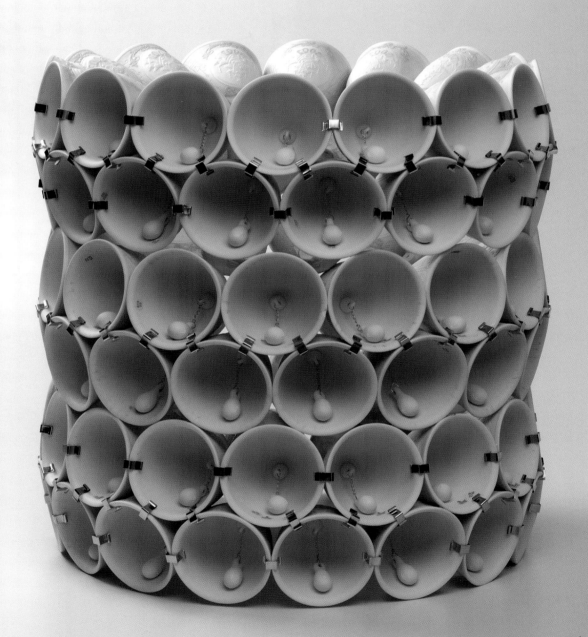

LLADRÓ (Re-cycled)
Cul de sac
Photo: Lladró / Re-cycled

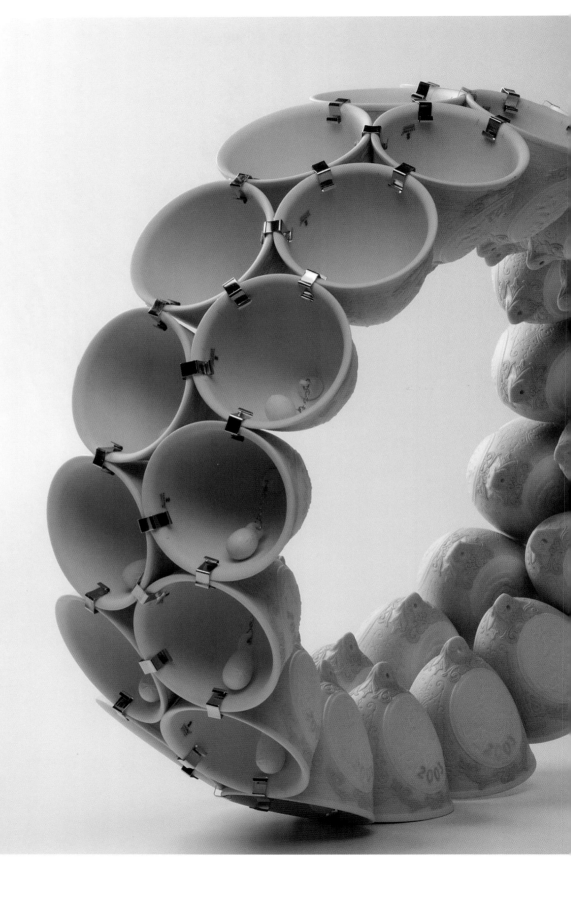

LLADRÓ (Re-cycled)
Cul de sac
Photo: Lladró / Re-cycled

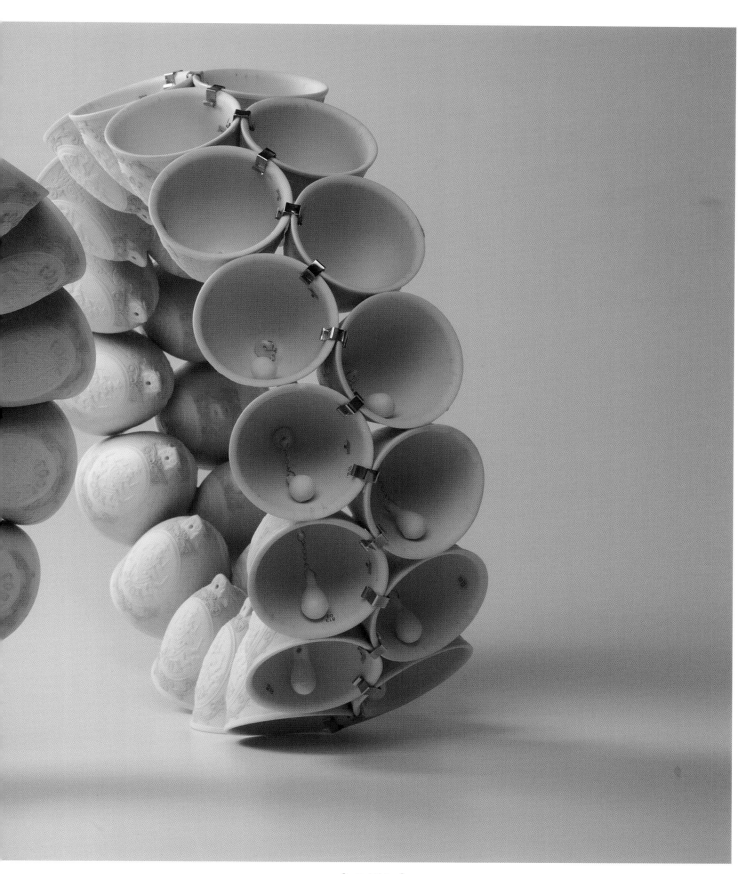

LACED FENCE 2005
Demakersvan

This project is a cross between compassion and hostility.
Industrial design and art are combined in such a natural way
demonstrating yet again that purely functional can also be
extremely decorative.
Expo Cologne 2006 IDEAL HOUSE.

Este proyecto es una mezcla de sensibilidad y de hostilidad.
Diseño industrial y arte se mezclan de forma muy natural
demostrando una vez más que la funcionalidad pura puede
ser muy decorativa.
Expo Cologne 2006 IDEAL HOUSE.

ANIMAUX
Big Game
Photo: Milo Séller

It is now possible to have a hunting trophy in your house without killing a single animal.
These revived and modernised trophies are made from sheets of wood and come in easy to assemble flat packs.

Materials: Beech wood.
Deer, 10cm x 17cm x 30cm
Stag, 52cm x 25cm x 70cm
American moose, 96cm x 62cmx 86cm
Made by Vlaemsch.
www.vlaemsch.be
Created at Ecal, Lausanne.

Ahora es posible disponer en su casa de un trofeo de caza sin matar un animal. Estos trofeos rejuvenecidos y modernizados hechos de láminas de madera son sencillos de montar por uno mismo y se llevan a casa en pequeños paquetes planos.

Materiales: Madera de haya.
Corzo, 10cm x 17cm x 30cm
Ciervo, 52cm x 25cm x 70cm
Alce de América 96cm x 62cmx 86cm
Fabricado por Vlaemsch.
www.vlaemsch.be
Creado en Ecal, Lausanne.

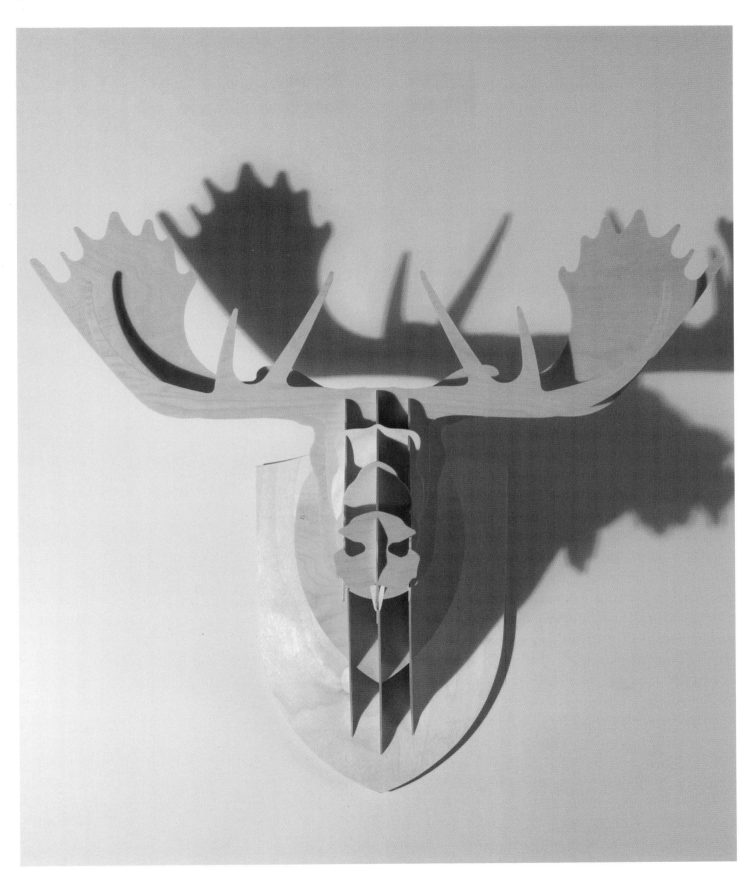

Still Life Fruit Bowl – 2005
Barnaby Bradford
Why spend millions on a Vermeer Picture when we can create our own still life at home with this fruit bowl and some seasonal fruit.

Porque gastarse millones en un cuadro de Vermeer cuando gracias a este frutero podemos crear en casa nuestro propio bodegón con fruta de temporada.

Next page / página siguiente
LA SIESTA
Cul de sac
Alberto Martínez (Cul de Sac), Hector Serrano and Raky Martínez
This white terracotta jug combines the appearance of a plastic water bottle with the advantages of a traditional earthenware "botijo" or drinking bottle. An alternative drinking vessel. With the growing preoccupation for a healthy balanced diet, we are led to think twice about the massive consumption of water in our homes, at work and in our free time which usually comes in plastic bottles. The challenge is to improve the water's quality whilst preserving its natural properties throughout the day using environmentally friendly materials.
Material: white terracotta.
Made by La Mediterránea.

Jarra realizada en terracota blanca que combina la apariencia de la botella de agua de plástico con las ventajas del tradicional botijo. Una forma diferente de beber. La creciente preocupación por llevar una alimentación sana y equilibrada, nos lleva a reflexionar sobre el consumo masivo de agua envasada en plástico y sobre el uso que hacemos de ella en casa, en el trabajo o en nuestro tiempo libre. El reto es mantener intactas sus propiedades y mejorar su condiciones durante todo el día, usando materiales ecológicos.
Materiales: terracota blanca
Producida por La Mediterránea.

BARROCO
Rosaria Rattin@Kose Milano
A series of designs made from traditional
handcrafted materials such as clay, wood
and gauze. These pure delicate designs
together with the manufacturing process
combine to create these unique and
precious pieces.

Serie de creaciones realizada de forma
artesanal utilizando materiales como la
arcilla, la madera y la gasa. Las formas
muy delicadas y puras y el proceso de
fabricación, hacen de estas creaciones
piezas únicas y preciosas.

HEATWAVE 2004
Joris Laarman
Radiator
Photo: Mathieu van Ek

HEATWAVE 2004
Joris Laarman
Radiator
Photo: Mathieu van Ek
This material used to create this wall radiator provides better heat transmission than the usual steel built alternatives as well as having a higher decorative value due to the ease with which it can be shaped.
A truly practical work of art.
Materials: concrete reinforced with fibre glass.
Produced and marketed by Droog Design.
www.droogdesign.nl

Los materiales utilizados proporcionan a este radiador mural una transmisión del calor más eficiente que los radiadores hechos de hierro además de darle un alto valor decorativo por la libertad de formas que permite.
Una verdadera obra de arte y de funcionalidad.
Materiales: cemento armado reforzado con fibra de vidrio.
Producido y comercializado por Droog Design.
www.droogdesign.nl

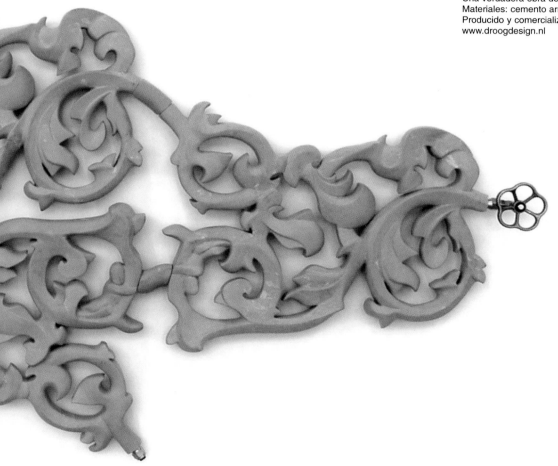

Flames 2003
Chris Kabel
Photo: Maarten van Houten
This three branch gas chandelier is sure to
add a touch of refined intimacy to any romantic
dinner for two or cosy get together with friends.
Colour: White RAL9016
Dimensions: 53cm x 23cm ø 11,5cm
Produced and marketed by Moooi.

Una cena romántica con el ser querido o con
amigos, este candelabro a gas de tres brazos
dará seguro un toque refinado e íntimo a su
reunión.
Color: Blanco RAL9016
Dimensiones: 53cm x 23cm ø 11,5cm
Producido y distribuido by Moooi.

CASPER CANDLE 2003
Tobias Wong
Chandelier
Thanks to its wick and glass paraffin
container, this chandelier is able to
provide hours of intimate lighting.

Gracias a su mecha y un depósito
de cristal de aceite de parafina, este
candelabro proporciona una íntima
luz durante horas.

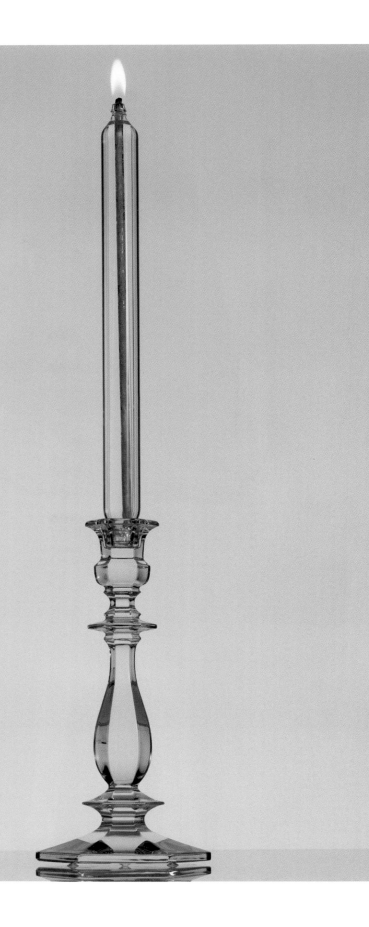

HUMANISTIC COLLECTOR 2005
Fréderic Ruyant
Reliquary .
With the appearance of a cross between the
Holy Grail and a space capsule.
Materials: níckel–plated brass.
Exposition Tools galerie, Paris 2005.

Relicario.
Con una estética a mitad de camino entre el
receptáculo sagrado y la cápsula espacial.
Materiales: latón niquelado.
Exposición Tools galerie, Paris 2005.

CONVERSATION PIECE 2002
Barnaby Bradford

"Conversation piece" is an aid to couples who usually remain silent throughout dinner. The legendary "Willow Pattern" was created 200 years ago by the English to boost the sales of ceramic ware. This romantic tale was drawn and painted on white ceramic plates with a phosphorescent finish, to be later read by couples, in turn encouraging a spark of love and passion.

"Conversation piece" es una ayuda para las parejas que se quedan en silencio durante la cena. "The willow Pattern" es una leyenda creada por los ingleses hace 200 años para promocionar la venta de cerámica. Este cuento fue dibujado y pintado en platos de cerámica blanca. Esta historia romántica puede ser leída por la pareja en estos platos fosforescentes, provocando tal vez, un chispazo de amor y pasión.

JEANNETTE & JACQUETTE
Iona Vautrin
Porcelain fruit bowl with integrated table mat.

Frutero con tapete integrado realizado en porcelana.

Nature

ARTIFICIAL PLANT
Frank Tjepkema@Tjep

Why try to mimic nature when it means creating artificial plants? Designers now have absolute powers of creation to invent currently non-existent varieties. An imitation often proves to be lamentable and vulgar whereas an original is always more beautiful and more realistic. At least this new artificial plant doesn't purport to be something it isn't.
Materials: rubber polyurethane and polypropylene.
Dimensions: 50cm x 50 cm
This creation is part of a permanent collection at the Centraal Museum in Utrecht.
Produced by Droog Design.

¿Porqué copiar la naturaleza cuando se trata de crear plantas artificiales?. Los diseñadores pueden tomarse el acto creativo como una libertad infinita, para crear plantas que no existen. La copia puede tener un resultado desafortunado y vulgar. El original es siempre más bonito y más real. Al menos esta nueva planta artificial no nos miente. No es real y no pretende serlo .
Materiales: poliuretano caucho y polipropileno,
Dimensiones: 50cm x 50 cm
Esta creación forma parte de la colección permanente del Centraal Museum en Utrecht.
Producido por Droog Design.

GRO
Joe and Janet Doucet@Intotonyc
Space divider system

The required configuration for a room divider is created by combining the two different shaped pieces (straight and curved). This system is inspired by the grass walls created by some African tribes.
Materials: white acrylic, fine green acrylic rods.
Dimensions:
Rods: 7.6cm ø 3mm
Straight base: 2.5cm x 35.6cm x 15.2cm
Curved base: 2.5cm x 17.8cm x 22.9cm

Combinando los dos tipos de piezas (rectas y curvadas) podemos crear la configuración deseada para separar un ambiente. Este sistema está inspirado en las paredes hechas de hierbas de algunas tribus africanas.
Materiales: acrílico blanco, barritas de acrílico verde.
Dimensiones:
Barritas: 7,6cm ø 3mm
Base recta: 2,5cm x 35,6cm x 15,2cm
Base curvada: 2,5cm x 17,8cm x 22,9cm

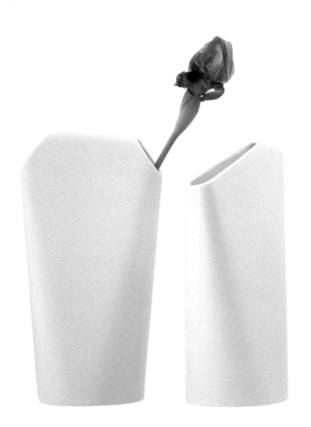

ONE CERAMIC 2000
Sebastian Bergne
Collection of vases.
Material: ceramic.
Made by Driade, D-House.

Familia de floreros.
Materiales: cerámica.
Producido por Driade, D-House.

MICROGARDEN 2005
Sebastian Bergne
Mini garden system.
Ideal for small urban spaces. These stackable flowerpots, designed to be used for decorative purposes, come in different sizes according to space and requirements.
Material: ceramic.
Made by Muji.

Ideal para espacios urbanos reducidos. Estas macetas son apilables y de diferentes tamaños para decorar según el espacio y las necesidades.
Materiales: cerámica.
Producido por Muji.

CHAPEAUX POUR VASE
Guillaume Delvigne

This vase consists of a single transparent glass base, the appearance of which can be changed by a range of fine ceramic accessories which adapt to the size of the bouquet of flowers.
Materials: glass and ceramic.

Compuesto de una única base de cristal transparente, este florero cambia de aspecto gracias a una serie de complementos de cerámica fina que se adaptan al tamaño del ramo de flores.
Materiales: vidrio y cerámica.

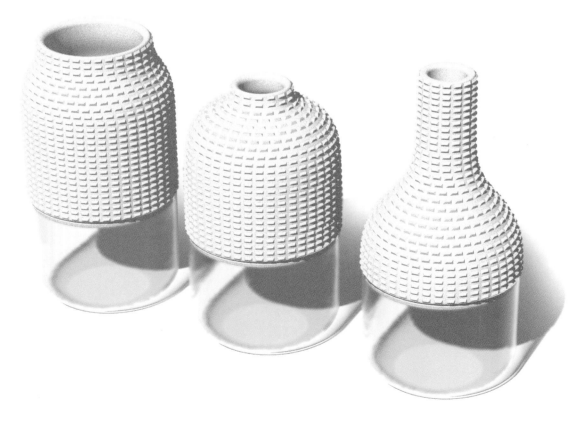

SPORE
Joe and Janet Doucet@Intotonyc
Ceramic vase

This vase is generated by turning nature upside down. Flowers contain pollen spores, but in this case the spores contain the flowers.
Materials: ceramic.
Dimensions: 30.5cm x 30.5cm x 30.5cm

Este florero ha nacido a partir de la idea de invertir el orden de la naturaleza. Las flores contienen esporas de polen, pero en este caso las esporas contienen flores.
Materiales: cerámica.
Dimensiones: 30,5cm x 30,5cm x 30,5cm

SQUARE VASE 1999
Ronan y Erwan Bouroullec
Photo: Morgane Le Gall
This peculiar square flower vase makes for a somewhat unusual flower arrangement. The design suggests that each branch is to be placed in a different hole, rather like the Ikebana concept.
Material: ceramic.
Dimensions: 5cm x 40cm x 40cm
Production: Cappellini.

Este peculiar florero de forma cuadrada invita a colocar las flores de un manera distinta. Los diferentes agujeros sugieren una colocación de los ramos uno por uno, siguiendo un poco el concepto del Ikebana.
Materiales: cerámica.
dimensiones: 5cm x 40cm x 40 cm
Producción: Cappellini.
www.cappellini.it

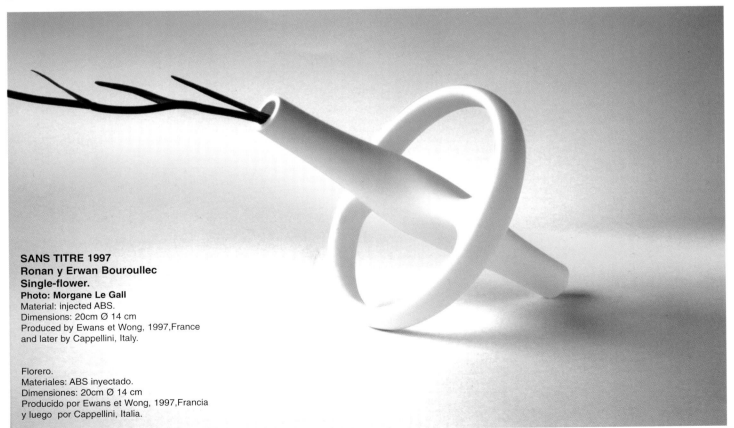

SANS TITRE 1997
Ronan y Erwan Bouroullec
Single-flower.
Photo: Morgane Le Gall
Material: injected ABS.
Dimensions: 20cm Ø 14 cm
Produced by Ewans et Wong, 1997,France
and later by Cappellini, Italy.

Florero.
Materiales: ABS inyectado.
Dimensiones: 20cm Ø 14 cm
Producido por Ewans et Wong, 1997,Francia
y luego por Cappellini, Italia.

FLOAT
Joe and Janet Doucet@Intotonyc
Porcelain bud vase.

This flower vase, inspired by a wine bottle floating in the sea, captures the tranquillity of the moment to perfection.
The angle of the bottle and its position create the illusion that the rest of the bottle is beneath the surface.
Material: Porcelain.
Dimensions: 11cm x 7.6cm

Inspirado en una botella de vino flotando en el mar, este florero parece capturar un momento de tranquilidad perfecta.
Su inclinación y su posición crean la ilusión de que el resto de la botella este debajo de la superficie.
Materiales: Porcelana.
Dimensiones: 11cm x 7,6cm

DESIGNED BY MOTION
Front design

A collection of "design by" objects created by the girls at Front design which leave natural factors to be the "designers". In this case, the object has been designed by movement. The dreaded fall which causes the flower vase to break is recreated by a number of vases each representing a stage of the fall. The result? A very original flower vase.

La serie de objetos "design by" creada por las chicas de Front design, dejan a los factores naturales ser los "diseñadores". En este caso el movimiento es el diseñador de este objeto. La caída temida que llevará el florero a romperse está figurada con varios floreros representando cada etapa de la trayectoria. ¿Resultado?. Un florero muy original.

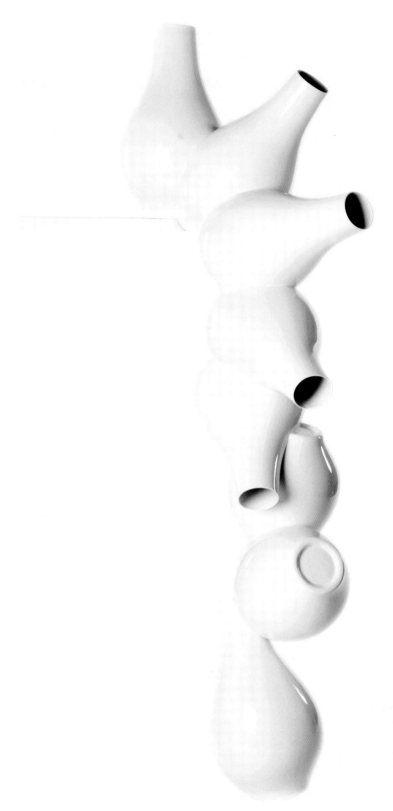

PLANT LIGHT 2005
Mikko Laakkonen@rehti
Photo: Timo Ryttäri

Material: aluminium.
Dimensions: 43 cm x 50 cm ø 22 cm
Prototype.

Materiales: aluminio.
Dimensiones: 43 cm x 50 cm ø 22 cm
Prototipo.

Streamgarden
Hans Andersson
& Johan Svensson@greenfortune
Photo: Peter Orevi

Thanks to Streamgarden, having a small garden either at home or in the office is within everyone's reach. These plastic flowerpots have an integrated hydroponics system which supports rapid growth and development by making the most efficient use of the water and nutrients. For those without green fingers when it comes to caring for plants, this system requires very little attention. All it needs is to check the water level and top up once a week. The water and nutrients have to be changed every three months. It only remains to decide what we would like to cultivate: flowers, tomatoes, cucumbers….

Gracias a Streamgarden, tener un pequeño jardín en casa o en la oficina está al alcance de todos. Estas macetas de plástico integran un sistema de cultivo hidropónico, que permite un crecimiento y desarrollo muy rápido, utilizando el agua y los nutrientes de la manera más eficaz. Para los que no tienen suerte con el cuidado de las plantas, este sistema no necesita mucha atención. Solo hace falta controlar el nivel y rellenar de agua una vez a la semana. El cambio de agua y de nutrientes se hace cada tres meses. Sólo nos queda por elegir lo que vamos a cultivar: flores, tomates, pepinos…

STONE VASE 2002
Ronan and Erwan Bouroullec
Photo: Paul Tahon

Flower vases commissioned by the "Délégation aux
Arts Plastiques". Ministry of Culture, France.
Material: porcelain.
Dimensions: 9cm x 16cm x 18cm

Floreros comisionados por la "Délégation aux
Arts Plastiques". Ministerio de cultura, de Francia
Materiales: porcelana.
Dimensiones: 9cm x 16cm x 18cm

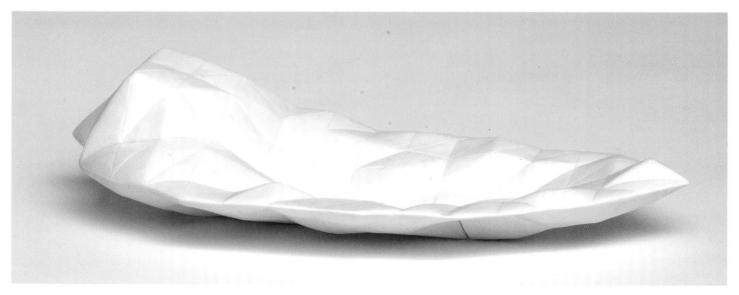

STONE BOWL 2002
Ronan and Erwan Bouroullec
Photo: Paul Tahon

Bowl commissioned by the "Délégation aux Arts
Plastiques", Ministry of Culture, France.
Material: porcelain.
Dimensions: 9 x 16 x 36 cm

Centro de mesa comisionado por la "Délégation aux Arts
Plastiques", Ministerio de cultura, Francia.
Materiales: porcelana.
Dimensiones:9 x 16 x 36 cm

COMBINATORY VASES 1998
Ronan and Erwan Bouroullec
Photo: Morgane Le Gall

The idea behind Combinatory vases is based on the production of eight pieces of injected moulded plastic which individually appear to have no apparent function but which come into their own collectively, combining to create an infinite number of objects. This ingenious way to create mass produced diversity allows the buyer to intervene in the creative process.
Material: polyurethane
Dimensions: variable
Produced by Néotu Gallery, 1997 France, and by Cappellini, Italy in 1998.

La idea de Combinatory vases está basada en la producción por inyección de plástico de ocho piezas que no tienen ninguna función aparente por separado, y que cumplen todo su sentido combinándose para crear una infinidad de productos. Una manera inteligente de crear diversidad en serie y de dejar intervenir al comprador en el proceso creativo.
Materiales: poliuretano
Dimensiones: variables
Producido por Néotu Gallery, 1997 France, y por Cappellini, Italy en 1998.

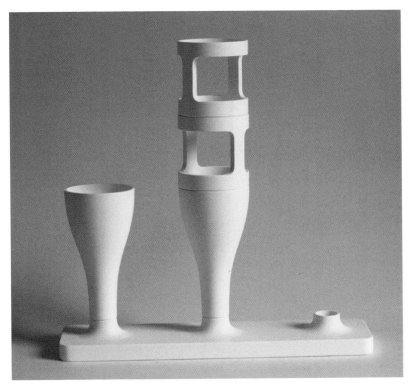

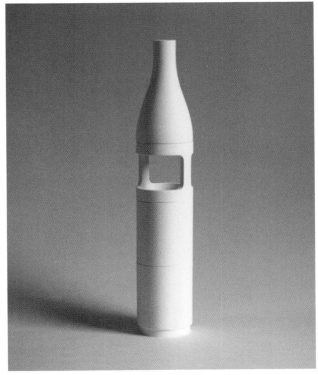

VERSO DIVERSO
Nicolas La Moigne

How to convert a simple plastic bottle into a designer object. It needs only to screw this ingenious piece to the bottle neck to either serve drinks at a party or to water the plants.
Winner of the MACEF DESIGN AWARD 2005 (International Design Competition, January 2005).
Adapts to fit all bottles currently available on the market.
Colours: orange, pink, green, blue and yellow.
Produced by Viceversa.

Como convertir una simple botella de plástico en objeto de diseño. Para servir bebidas durante una fiesta o para regar las plantas, solo hace falta enroscar este ingenioso objeto al cuello de la botella.
Premiado en MACEF DESIGN AWARD 2005 (International Design Competition, Enero 2005).
Adaptable a todas las botellas disponibles en el mercado.
Colores: naranja, rosa, verde, azul y amarillo.
Producido por Viceversa.

CERAMIC VASE 2004
Nicolas Le Moigne
Watering can / Vase
Once the flower dies, the vase becomes a watering can, using the water which remains inside.
Material: ceramic.
Dimensions / 16.5cm x 28cm x 11cm
Self produced.

Regadora / jarrón
Una vez que la flor se muere, el jarrón se convierte en regadora utilizando el agua que se ha quedado dentro.
Materiales: cerámica.
Dimensiones/ 16,5cm x 28cm x 11cm
Producción propia.

TROMPE L'ÓEIL 2005
Nicolas Le Moigne
The practical solution to create an original vase from a glass.
Material: enamelled metal.
Dimensions: 17cm x 10cm
Produced by Banal Extra.
www.banalextra.it

La solución práctica para obtener unl jarrón a partir de un vaso.
Materiales: metal esmaltado.
Dimensiones: 17cm x 10cm
Producido por BanalExtra
www.banalextra.it

 Exhibited at / Expuesto en:
100%Design, Tokyo Design Week 2005
International Contemporary Furniture Fair (ICFF), Nueva York 2005, Maison & Objet, París, 2005.

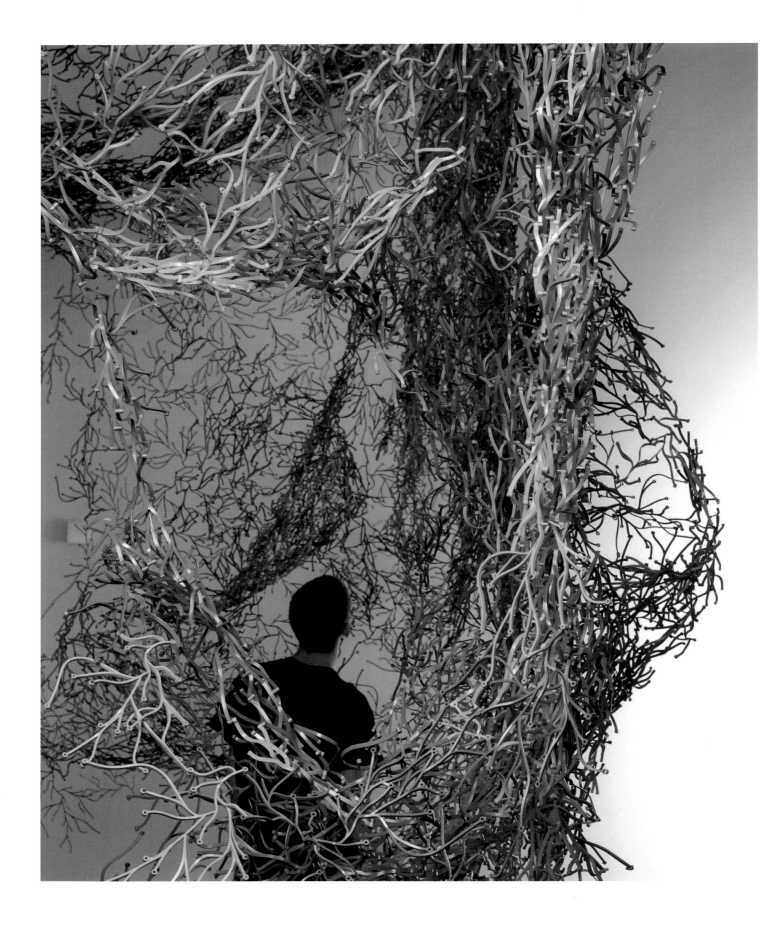

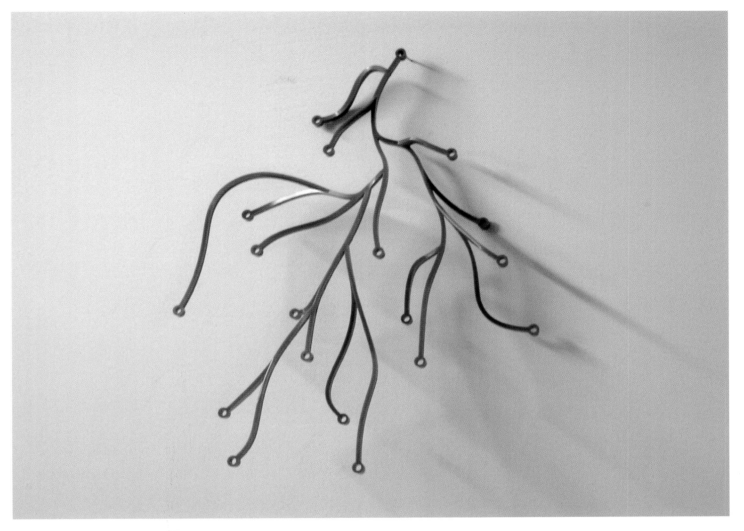

ALGUES 2004
Ronan and Erwan Bouroullec
Photo: Paul Tahon
Plastic seaweed.
Material: injected polypropylene.
Dimensions: 27cm x 23cm x 4cm
Made by Vitra (International).
www.vitra.com

Alga de plástico.
Materiales: polipropileno inyectado.
Dimensiones: 27cm x 23cm x 4cm
Fabricado por Vitra (International).
www.vitra.com

Roubaix exhibition 2004
Location / Instalación:
"La Piscine, Musée d'art et d'industrie
de Roubaix, France".

Airco Tree for the British Airways executive lounge.
Frank Tjepkema & Janneke Hooymans

Designed to give meaning and significance to the air conditioning duct in the British Airways first class executive lounge at Heathrow airport. The ducting was approximately the same size as a tree trunk apart from at the top, which extended from between two to six metres. The comparison between this metal ducting and a tree prove to be quite attractive and comforting. The lounge has been transformed into a village square with the tree in the centre symbolising a meeting place and just as the tree provides oxygen, the air-conditioning unit provides the lounge's occupants with fresh air. The general shape of this tree has been generated by a partial transformation of graphic profiles taken from tree branches. The resulting huge dynamic structure completely disguises the protruding equipment.

Client: Droog Design for British Airways.
Located in Terminal 1 at Heathrow airport (London).
Winner of the interior design category in the 2004 "Dutch Design" awards.

Se trataba de dar sentido y significado al tubo de aire acondicionado del salón de ejecutivo de primera clase de British Airways, en el aeropuerto de Heathrow. El tubo tenía las dimensiones aproximadas de un tronco de árbol excepto la altura, que ampliaron de dos a seis metros. La comparación de este tubo metálico con un árbol resultó muy atractiva y cómoda. La sala se convertía en una plaza de pueblo, con el árbol en medio como un símbolo de punto de encuentro. Además tal como un árbol provee oxigeno, el climatizador proporciona aire fresco a los ocupantes de la sala. Las formas generales de este árbol simbólico han sido generadas por una revolución parcial de perfiles gráficos de ramas de árbol. El resultado monumental y muy dinámico, hace desaparecer por completo la protuberancia de la maquinaria.

Cliente: Droog Design para British Airways.
Se sitúa en la terminal 1 del aeropuerto de Heathrow (Londres).
Ganador del "Dutch Design" Awards en el 2004, categoría diseño de interior.

URBAN OASIS
Editions Jean-Michel Place. Paris, 2004
Frederic Ruyant

Public spaces, supermarket car parks, façades and bus stops are transformed into settings for incongruous, poetic events, in an attempt to reinvent the city. These acts and projects make us want to believe that the urban environment is not simply a desert for mankind.

Espacios públicos, aparcamientos de supermercado, fachadas, paradas de autobús, se convierten en teatros de eventos incongruentes, poéticos, como unas propuestas para reinventar la ciudad. Son actos y proyectos que nos dan ganas de creer que el espacio urbano no es un desierto para el hombre.

GUN VASES
Suck UK
Flower vases
Model 1 table top
Model 2 wall fixing.
Demonstrating a more pacific use for
arms. The power created by the
aesthetics of arms.
Material: ceramic.

Floreros
Modelo 1 sobremesa
Modelo 2 fijación en la pared.
Por un uso más pacífico de la armas.
La fuerza de la estética de las armas.
Material: cerámica.

SIGNATURE VASES
Joris Laarman and Frank Tjepkema

"Signature Vase" is not simply another vase. These flower vases are unique and designed directly from written signatures, the profiles of which provide the basis for the simple extrusion.
Material: Nylon.
Dimensions: approx: 30cm x 20cm x 25cm
This project is a tribute to Ron Arad for his forward thinking work in the field of stereo-lithography.
Produced by Droog Design.

"Signature Vase" no es un florero más. Estos floreros son únicos y diseñados directamente a partir de firmas escritas cuyos perfiles sirven de base a una simple extrusión.
Materiales: Nylon.
Dimensiones: aprox: 30cm x 20cm x 25cm
Este proyecto es un homenaje a Ron Arad y su vanguardista trabajo en el campo de la estereolitografía.
Producido por Droog Design.

PureTech

EXTERNAL INFRARED RAYS UNIT 2004
Toshihiko Sakai@Sakai Design Associate.

COMPROJECTOR 2004
Toshihiko Sakai@Sakai Design Associate
Projector H125mm.
Proyector H125mm.
Prototype / Prototipo.

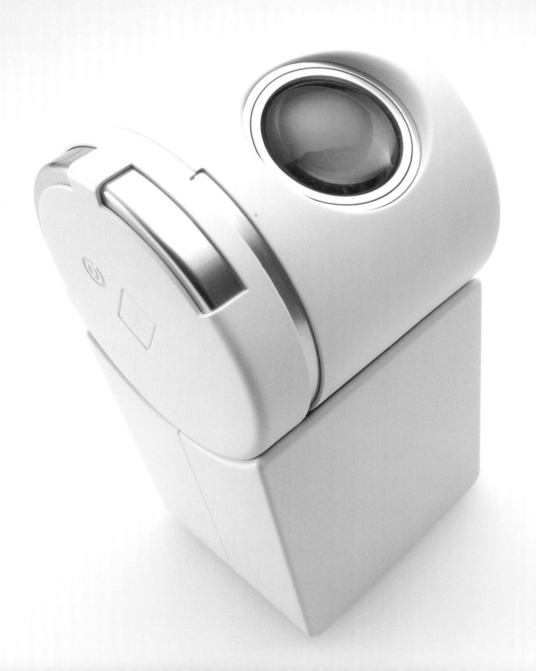

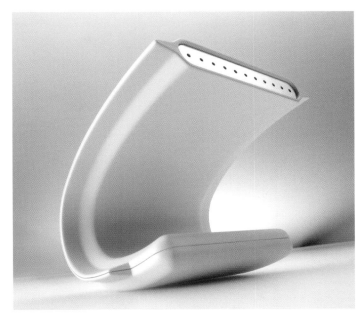

COMMIC 2004
Toshihiko Sakai@Sakai Design Associate
Microphone / micrófono.
Prototype / prototipo.

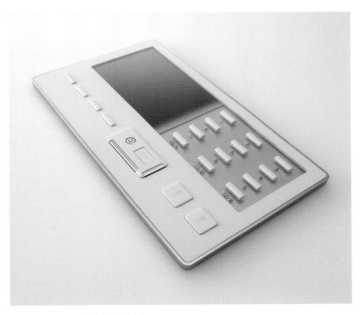

BUILD-IN REMOCOM 2004
Toshihiko Sakai@Sakai Design Associate
Cordless wall control panel.
Panel de control de pared inalámbrico.
Prototype / prototipo.

COMCAMERA2004
Toshihiko Sakai@Sakai Design Associate
Digital camera.
Cámara digital.
Prototype / prototipo.

COMTAP ComChecker 2004
Toshihiko Sakai@Sakai Design Associate
Intelligent Tap, Wireless Electric Current Checkers.
Enchufes de corriente eléctrica Inalámbricos.
Prototype / prototipo.

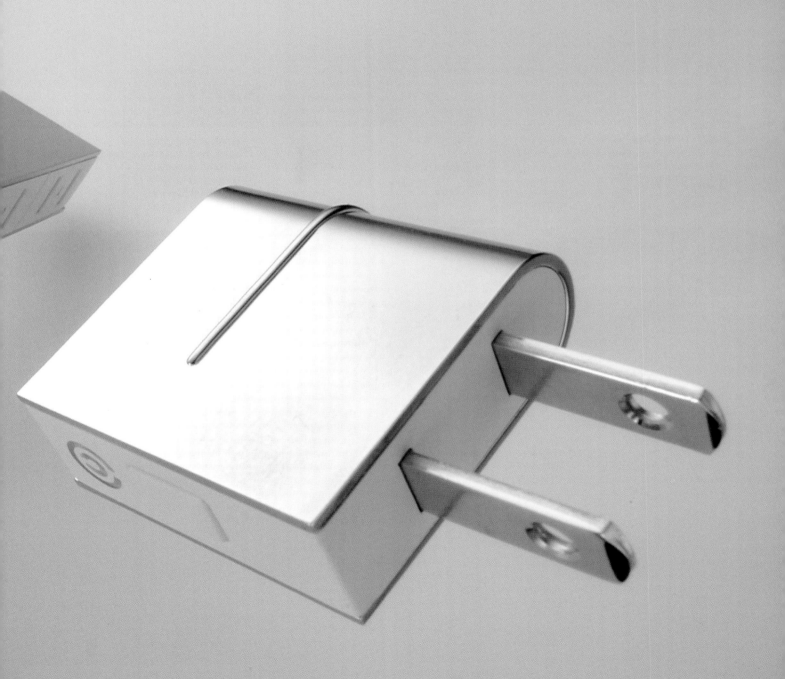

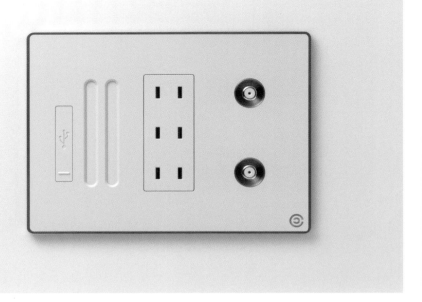

COMSTATION Internal Triple 2004
Toshihiko Sakai@Sakai Design Associate
Wall Mounted Home Server
Enchufe de pared multi-función.
Prototype / prototipo.

SWITCHREMOCOM 2004
Toshihiko Sakai@Sakai Design Associate
intelligent Switch-Plate.
Interruptor inteligente.
Prototype / prototipo.

COMDISPLAY 2004
Toshihiko Sakai@Sakai Design Associate
15inch LCD screen.
Pantalla LCD 15inch.
Prototype / portotipo.

1. Pastorale siciliana
2. Tarantella napoletana
3. Il carnevale di Venezia
4. U cchiu' beddu diamanti
5. Gran valzer
6. Controdanza
7. Mi votu e mi rivotu -violin solo
8. La traviata -Preludio all'atto 1
9. Taormina···si bedda tu
10. Torna a Surriento
11. Passeggiando per Lipari
12. Mi votu e mi rivotu
13. Cavalleria rusticana-Intermezzo
14. Vitti'na crozza

CD PLAYER 1999
MUJI
This CD player, designed exclusively for MUJI, comes from the "without thought" workshop. Initially it wasn't actually designed for mass market production and with its minimalist appearance it looks more like a mini fan with the cable as the on/off switch. The speakers are integrated into the body of the piece itself with the control buttons on the upper spine. From being sold originally as a limited edition for MUJI Europe, it is now on a massive production line to meet unprecedented demand.
In addition to its public success this CD player has also received a number of awards:
Product of outstanding design at the 2002 Japanese Design awards.
Design Week: Best consumer product 2002.
IF Hanover Gold Award 2002.
Dimensions: 17cm x 17cm x 4cm
Colours: black or white.

Diseñado exclusivamente para la marca MUJI, este CD player nació del workshop "without thought". Al principio no fue destinado a la producción industrial. Con una estética muy minimalista, se parece más a un mini ventilador con su cable que funciona como interruptor on/off. Los altavoces están integrados al cuerpo del objeto y los botones de mando están situados en el lomo superior. Pasó de ser vendido en edición limitada en Muji Europa a una producción masiva gracias a una gran demanda sin precedentes.
Además del éxito de publicó, ganó varios premios:
Product of outstanding design' at the 2002 Japanese Design awards.
Design Week: Best consumer product 2002.
IF Hanover Gold Award 2002.
Dimensiones: 17cm x 17cm x 4cm
Colores: blanco o negro.

Precious

Bling Bling medallion 2002
Frank Tjepkema@Tjep

In the designer's words:

"This medallion is the object bearing the most brand names in the world. Imagine the money that you will be able to save in clothing by simply wearing this one piece of jewellery!"

Seen from a distance it appears to be a cross. Close up we can see a fine superimposed layer of logos from famous international designer houses. A new religious symbol for the capitalist consumerism elite?

This piece of jewellery is from the permanent collection at the "Stedelijk Museum" in Ámsterdam and the "Museum 't Kruithuis". Bling Bling was nominated for the "Rotterdam Design Prize 2003" and was winner of the fashion design category in the 2004 "Dutch Design Awards".

Materials: Silver and gold.

Dimensions: 8cm x 9cm

Su creador dice:

"Este medallón es el objeto que más marcas tiene en el mundo. ¡Imaginaros el dinero que vais a poder ahorrar en ropa de marca solo llevando esta joya!"

Visto de lejos es una cruz. De cerca nos damos cuenta de la fina superposición de capas de logotipos de famosas marcas internacionales. Un Nuevo símbolo religioso para adeptos al consumismo capitalista?

Esta joya es parte de la colección permanente del "Stedelijk Museum" de Ámsterdam y del "Museum 't Kruithuis". Bling Bling fue nominado para el "Rotterdam Design Prize 2003" y ha sido ganador del "Dutch Design Awards" en el 2004 en la categoría diseño de moda.

Materiales: Plata u oro.

Dimensiones: 8cm x 9cm

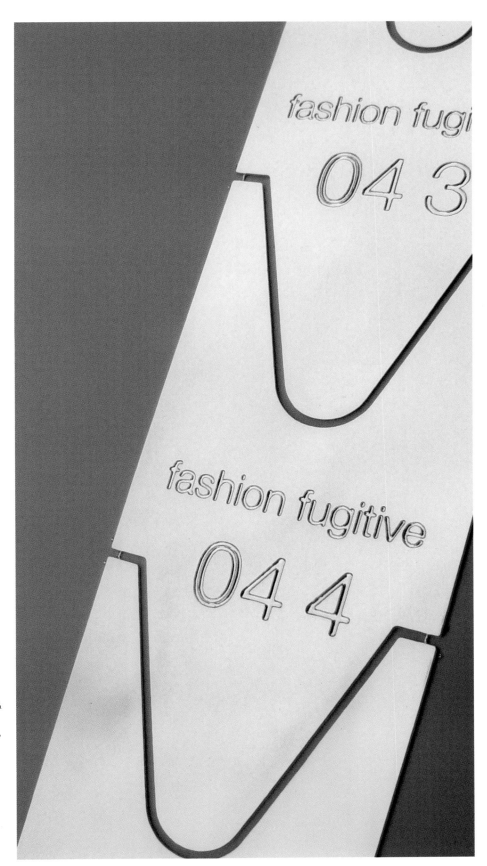

FASHION FUGITIVE DISTINCTION 2002
Henk van Dijke and Frank Tjepkema
A joint project between Eddy Schennink & Marieke
Schooneman from Hello for Fashion Fugitives.
Fashion fugitives are the opposite of "fashion victims".
A creative exercise to come up with some form of
"recompense" for non "fashion victims". However,
recompensing a non fashion victim with something visible
such as a medal automatically creates a "fashion
statement" and consequently a victim of that said
statement. In search of an object so banal that nobody
would be willing to sport it, we found one which coverts
everybody into a number.
The customary ticket at the meat counter queue!
Limited Edition.
Material: gold.
Dimensions: 4mm x 5cm

Proyecto realizado en colaboración con Eddy Schennink &
Marieke Schooneman de Hello para Fashion Fugitives.
Fashion fugitives es el contrario de "fashion victims".
Ejercicio creativo para idear una especie de "recompensa"
para los que no son "fashion victims". Sin embargo,
recompensando a una no-fashion victim con algo visible
como una medalla, se crea automáticamente un "fashion
statement" y como consecuencia una victima de ella.
Buscando un objeto de lo mas banal que nadie quisiera
lucir, encontraron uno que nos convierte a todos en un
número.
¡El típico tiquet de espera de la carnicería!.
Edición Limitada.
Materiales: oro.
Dimensiones: 4mm x 5cm

CRYSTAL BUBBLE WRAP
Klara Zavadilova@ECAL
The aim of this exercise was to create new uses for the famous Swarovski crystal. One unusual proposal transforms this familiar packaging material into a surprise jewellery box, inviting us to burst the bubbles and retrieve its precious contents.

Inventar nuevas utilizaciones del famoso cristal de Swarovski era la finalidad del ejercicio creativo. Una respuesta sorprendente que hace de este papel de embalaje un inesperado joyero invitándonos a romper las burbujas y recuperar el precioso contenido.

TAPE IT!
Adrien Rovero & Augustin Scott de Martinville@ECAL
The proposal put forward by these two designers:
The transformation of simple adhesive tape into a luxury item.
Adhesive tape encrusted with Swarovski crystals.

La respuesta de estos dos diseñadores:
La transformación de una simple cinta adhesiva en un objeto de
lujo. Cinta adhesiva incrustada de cristales Swarovski.

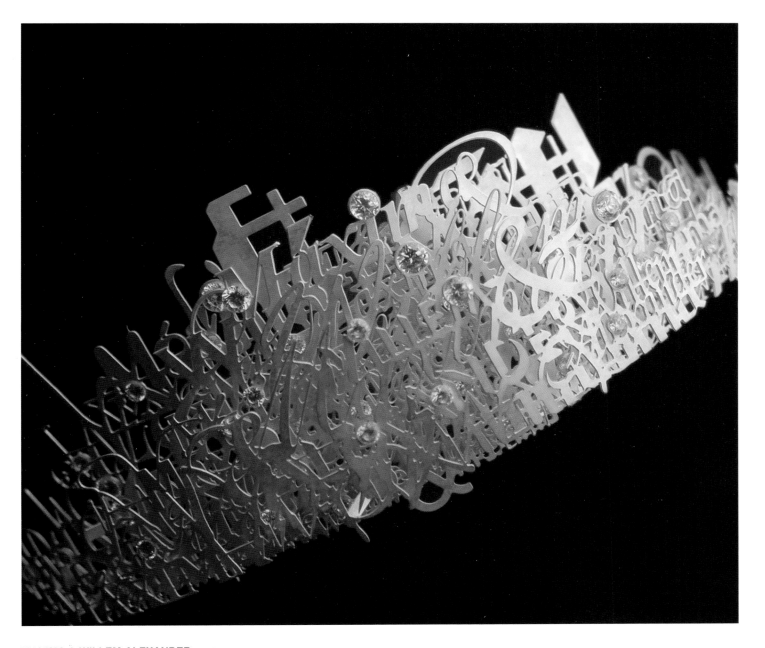

MAXIMA & WILLEM-ALEXANDER
& diamonds 2002

A tiara created for Maxima on the occasion of her wedding.
"Maxima & Willem-Alexander" is written in more than 100
different typographic fonts, creating a delicate and
extremely original decorative motif. However, not forgetting
what constitutes a girl's best friend, each letter "i" is dotted
with a diamond.
Created for an exhibition and competition organised by the
Muse Kruithuis in s'Hertogenbosch for the Royal Family in
the Netherlands.
Frank Tjepkema received an honorable mention.
This piece is now part of a permanent collection displayed
in the "Museum 't Kruithuis".
Materials: Silver and diamonds.
Dimensions: 14cm x 5.5cm
Produced by Tjep.

Tiara para la boda de Maxima.
"Maxima & Willem-Alexander" está escrito con mas de 100
fuentes tipográficas, creando un motivo muy delicado y
original. Pero no se tenía que olvidar quienes son los
mejores amigos de las mujeres. Cada punto sobre las "i"
son diamantes. Creado para una exposición y un concurso
organizado por el Muse Kruithuis en s'Hertogenbosch para
la Familia Real de los Paises Bajos.Frank Tjepkema
obtuvo la mención honorífica.
Esta pieza es parte de la colección permanente del
"Museum 't Kruithuis".
Materiales: plata y diamantes
Dimensiones: 14cm x 5,5 cm
Producido por Tjep.

JUSTICE
Divinas palabras
Justicia poética.
Photo: Inocuo Design Studio and Ojo por ojo.
Materials: Gold-plated 925 silver star brooch with a
surgical steel clasp and bas-relief inscription.
Made by Karatnia.

Materiales: Broche estrella en plata 925 con baño de
oro. Aguja en acero quirúrgico. Inscripción en bajo
relieve.
Realizada por Karatnia.

DIAMANTE EN BRUTO
Divinas palabras
Photo: Inocuo Design Studio and Ojo por ojo.
Materials: Rhodium plated white polished gold ring, laser engraved on the inside and inset with 11 uncut crystallised cubic diamonds. The diamonds, being uncut, are all unique and by carat, there being no two alike.
Made by Karatnia.

La belleza en estado puro. El diamante en bruto.
Materiales: Anillo de oro blanco pulido con baño de rodio y grabado láser en interior, con 11 diamantes en bruto de cristalización cúbica. Los diamantes, al no estar tallados, son piezas de kilataje y forma únicas, no hay dos iguales.
Realizada por Karatnia.

INDEPENDANCE, ENGAGEMENT.
Divinas palabras
Photo: Inocuo Design Studio and Ojo por ojo.

Independence and compromise are both equally
important in a caring relationship, to be treated
with equal respect so that neither one eclipses the
other. The two preserve their respective identities,
brought together by love to share a common
space.

Materials:
Twin rings which rotate up to a point. One 18 carat
gold ring fitted into another one in matt 316-L steel.
Made by Karatnia.

Alianza matrimonial

La independencia y el compromiso son
igualmente importantes en una relación amorosa,
en la que nadie se pierde en el otro. Los dos
mantienen su identidad y se encuentran en un
espacio común mediante el amor.

Materiales:
Anillo en doble aro con sistema de giro y tope.
Un aro en oro de 18 kilates encajado sobre otro
en acero 316-L mate.
Realizada por Karatnia.

GOLD INSIDE
PLATINIUM INSIDE
Tobias Wong
Diamond ring / anillo con diamante.

SWELL
Joe and Janet Doucet@intotonyc
The value of a ring is often considered to be in relation to the inset stone. This ring incorporates a subtle swelling which symbolizes a stone, doing away with the need for a diamond.

El valor de un anillo está muchas veces considerado en relación con la piedra que lleva. Este anillo tiene una sutil deformación simbolizando la piedra. No necesita diamante.

AKA KILLER RING
Tobias Wong

GOLDEN SPOON 01
Just Another Rich Kid and Tobias Wong
18k gold-plated.
Made by citizen-citizen.

Bañado en oro 18k.
Editado por citizen-citizen.

www.citizen-citizen.com

MURDURED (Skull Pendant)
Just Another Rich Kid and Tobias Wong
18k gold-plated chain and pendant .
Made by citizen-citizen.

Cadena y pendiente bañado en oro 18k.
Editado por citizen-citizen.

www.citizen-citizen.com

GOLD PILLS 2005
Just Another Rich Kid and Tobias Wong
24 carat gold capsules. 24 hour brilliance.
Transforms those "solid" needs into gold. The gold capsule
passes through the body, its journey's end being the toilet
bowl! Who was it that said it was all down to design?
Produced by citizen-citizen

Oro de 24k encapsulado.
24 horas brillantes. Transformará sus necesidades "sólidas"
en oro. El oro pasa directamente por el cuerpo y acabará su
peculiar camino en el aseo.
¿quién dice que todo ha sido diseñado?

Editado por citizen-citizen
www.citizen-citizen.com

SWIZZLE STICKS
Just Another Rich Kid and Tobias Wong
Solid gold 1970's Playboy drinks stirrers
18k gold-plated.
Issued by citizen-citizen.

Bañado en oro 18k.
Editado por citizen-citizen.

www.citizen-citizen.com

GOLDEN SPOON 02
Just Another Rich Kid and Tobias Wong
18k gold-plated.
Made by citizen-citizen.

Bañado en oro 18k.
Editado por citizen-citizen.

www.citizen-citizen.com

Pure furniture

Relax

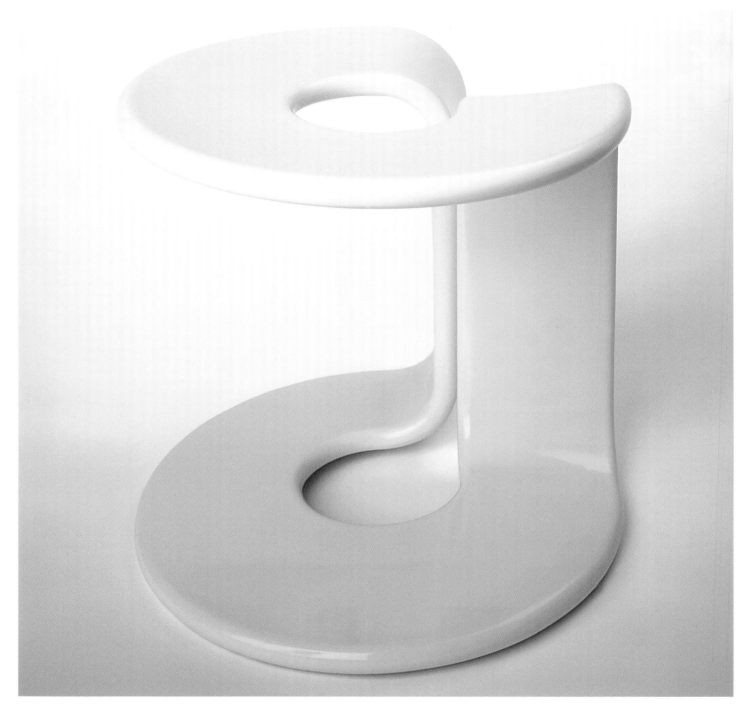

HALO
Joe and Janet Doucet@intotonyc
This stool is created by a single continuous contour making it a
visually interesting piece from any angle. The stool integrates just
as well into the home, café or gallery.
Dimensiones: 44.5cm x 44.5cm x 43.2cm

Este taburete está generado por una sola curva continua que lo
hace visualmente muy interesante desde cualquier punto de
vista. Se puede integrar perfectamente en casa, en un café o en
una galería.
Dimensiones: 44,5cm x 44,5cm x 43,2cm

WIDE ARMCHAIR 2004
Aleksi Penttilä@Rehti

Armchair.
Materials: stainless steel, Dibond.
(a composite panel made up of a resin core twice laminated both sides with 0.3mm thick aluminium).
Dimensions: 73.5 cm x 75 cm x 73.5 cm.
Prototype.

Sillón.
Materiales: acero inoxidable, Dibond.
(panel composite constituido por dos láminas de aleación de aluminio de 0,3 mm de espesor en ambas caras y un núcleo de resinas).
Dimensiones: 73,5 cm x 75 cm x 73,5 cm.
Prototipo.

IO
Joe and Janet Doucet@intotonyc
Leather lounge chair
According to Greek mythology, Zeus fell in love with a young mortal named Io. Hera, the wife of Zeus, upon hearing of the relationship transformed Io into a white cow. The leather on this chair may have even come from this very cow.
The chair, an excellent piece of craftsmanship, is made up of pieces of individually cut leather stitched with the same technique as used in saddle making.
Materials: Stainless steel frame and padova leather.
Dimensions: 68.5cm x 63.5cm x 76.2cm

Según la mitología griega, Zeus se enamoró de una joven mortal llamada Io. Al darse cuenta de esta relación, Hera, la mujer de Zeus, convirtió a Io en una vaca blanca. El cuero de esta silla, hubiera podido venir de la piel de esa vaca.
Está realizada por excelentes artesanos, con piezas de cuero Cortadas una por una y cosidas con la misma técnica empleada para coser las sillas de montar a caballo.
Materiales: base de acero inoxidable y cuero.
Dimensiones: 68,5cm x 63,5cm x 76,2cm

WELCOME
Cul de sac

This chair has been specially designed for
BonEstil, the company which mainly produces
articles manufactured from PUR. This material
and its technical properties are crucial and have
been exploited to the full in the creative
process. The resulting chair design is not only
surprising but original with dynamic yet soft
inviting lines.
Materials: Injected PUR.

Esta silla ha sido diseñada para la empresa
BonEstil que se dedicaba principalmente a la
fabricación de piezas en PUR. Este material y
sus características técnicas han sido muy
importantes y llevados hasta el limite durante el
proceso creativo. El resultado es sorprendente
y muy original. Una silla dinámica con unas
formas muy suaves y acogedoras.
Materiales: PUR inyectado.

SPIRO Taburete 2003
Herme Cisar & Mónica García@hermeymonica
This stool is made from a single rolled sheet of die-cut polypropylene.
Materials: 3mm polypropylene sheet.
Dimensions: 30cm x 30cm x 43cm
300cm x 100cm x 0.3cm unrolled.

Este taburete esta hecho de una sola lamina de polipropileno troquelada
y enrollada.
Materiales: lámina de polipropileno de 3mm.
Dimensiones: 30cm x 30cm x 43cm
300cm x 100cm x 0,3cm desplegado.

LA CHOSE 2003
Cédric Ragot

Stool.
"La Chose" according to its creator, is the outcome from
the genetic manipulation of an animal gene incorporated
within the genetic sequence of a stool.
Material: Polypropylene.
Exhibited at the "Salon du Meuble de Paris"
and in the Design Lab 2004.
Made by Obvious.

Taburete.
"La Chose" según su autor, es el resultado de una
manipulación genética de un gen animal incluido en una
secuencia genética de un taburete.
Materiales: Polipropileno.
Expuesto en el "Salon du Meuble de Paris".
y en Design Lab 2004.
Fabricado por Obvious.

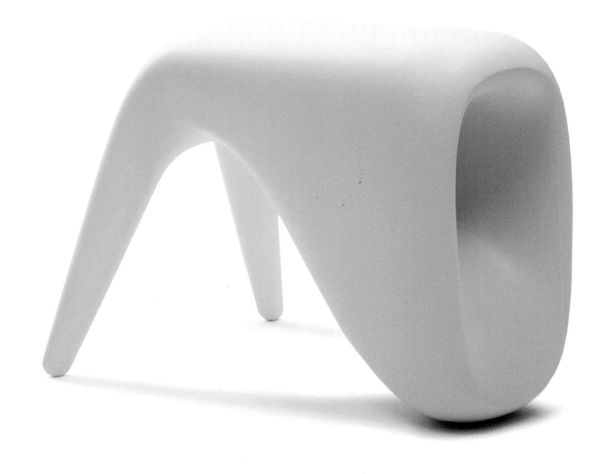

REST IN PEACE 2004
Robert Stadler
Photo: Patrick Gries.
Transformed garden chair.
This chair is the future skeleton of the most
invasive object on earth.
Dimensions: 87cm x 47cm x 40cm
A unique piece: Galerie Dominique Fiat, Paris.

Silla de jardín transformada.
Esta silla es el esqueleto del objeto más invasor
del planeta, encontrado en el futuro.
Dimensiones: 87cm x 47cm x 40cm
Pieza única : Galerie Dominique Fiat, París.

PILOW
Cul de sac

Stool designed for NEXUS.
A simple yet attractive design. The padded seat on Pilow is fully interchangeable thanks to the opening and closing mechanism making a variety of options possible.

Taburete diseñado para NEXUS.
Una visión simple y sugestiva. Gracias a su mecanismo de apertura y cierre, el asiento acolchado del cual presume Pilow es intercambiable, lo que facilitará mucho las cosas.

CHAIRS
Front design

With the aid of these black leather covers, we can now transform a simple garden chair into an indoor version with a rather more sophisticated touch.

Gracias a estas fundas de cuero negro, podemos transformar un simple silla de jardín en otra de interior con un toque más sofisticado.

TAK
Frank Tjepkema & Janneke Hooymans
we can now relax like birds in a nest thanks to
this sofa made from 50 soft rubber twigs. If the
family grows, so does the sofa by adding a few
more twigs. This nest sofa was specially created
for the Milan 2004 furniture exhibition.
Material: rubber.

Ahora podemos descansar como pájaros gracias
a este sofá hecho con 50 ramos de caucho
blando. Si la familia crece, el sofá también,
añadiéndole unos ramos más. Este sofá nido ha
sido creado para el salón del mueble de Milán
2004.
Materiales: caucho.

SOFT WOODEN
Front design
Photo: Anna Lönnerstam
This bench, of an apparently very simple form has the peculiarity of preserving an impression of the shape of the person who has been sat on top.
Material: wood.

Este banco de forma muy simple tiene la particulari-dad de guardar la silueta de la persona que se ha sentado encima.
Materiales: madera.

GRAPE CARPET
Ronan and Erwan Bouroullec
Photo: Paul Tahon.
Pure wool plush carpet, stitched in
one piece.
Colours: blue, green or grey.
Kreo Gallery, Paris.

Alfombra de pura lana aterciopelada,
cosida en una sola pieza.
Colores: azul, verde o gris.
Kreo Gallery, París.

PARASOL LUMINEUX 2001
Ronan and Erwan Bouroullec
Photo: Morgane Le Gall

Luminous parasol.
Materials: fibre glass, with a circular metal base.
Colour: white.
Light: 2 florescent lighting tubes with shade.
Dimensions: 200 x 186 x 186cm
Kreo Gallery, Paris.

Sombrilla luminosa.
Materiales: fibra de cristal, base circular de metal.
Color: blanco.
Luz: 2 tubos fluorescente con pantalla.
Dimensiones: 200 x 186 x 186 cm
Kreo Gallery, París.

AUDIOLAB 3, 2003
Laurent Massaloux

Photo: Laurent Massaloux.
Furniture purposely designed for listening to audio compositions. The set is made up of two swinging hammocks, a bedside table and a carpet. Both hammocks are equipped with 8 speakers emitting sound from the seat and the top.
Materials:
Epoxy painted frame.
Top: resin, acoustic equipment, speakers
Seat frame: wood, speakers.

Mobiliario dedicado a la escucha de obras sonoras. La instalación se compone de dos balancines de una mesita y de una alfombra. Cada balancín está equipado de 8 alta voces emitiendo el sonido desde el asiento y el techo.
Materiales:
Estructura de acero pintura epoxy.
Techo: resina, tela acústica, altavoces,
Estructura del asiento: madera, tela altavoces.

Production / Producción:
Caisse des Dépôts / MUDAM, Paris 2003
Collection / Collección:
MUDAM (Musée d'Art Moderne Grand Duc Jean),
Luxemburg.

Curators: Jean-Yves Leloup et Hervé Mikaeloff
Acoustics designer: Thierry Balasse
Participating soundtrack artists: David Toop , Thomas Brinkmann, Franck Scurti, Sutekh, The Customers, AGF, Domotic, Rebecca Bournigault.

SHADOW CHAIRS
Tanya Aguiñiga
This set of table and chairs are produced by a trick of light. Pieces of "half furniture" are fixed to the wall and become "whole" as a result of the illusion created by shadows, albeit it only for a very short time, when the light is at exactly the right angle.
Materials: Steel, medium density fibreboard.
Dimensions: 121.9cm x 101.6cm x 50.8cm

Esta serie de sillas y mesa juegan con la luz. Estos "medio muebles" se fijan en una pared y se convierten en objetos "enteros" gracias a las sombras creadas solamente durante unos instantes, cuando la luz del día está en el ángulo exacto para crear la ilusión.
Materiales: Acero, panel de fibras de madera de densidad media.
Dimensiones: 121,9cm x 101,6cm x 50,8cm

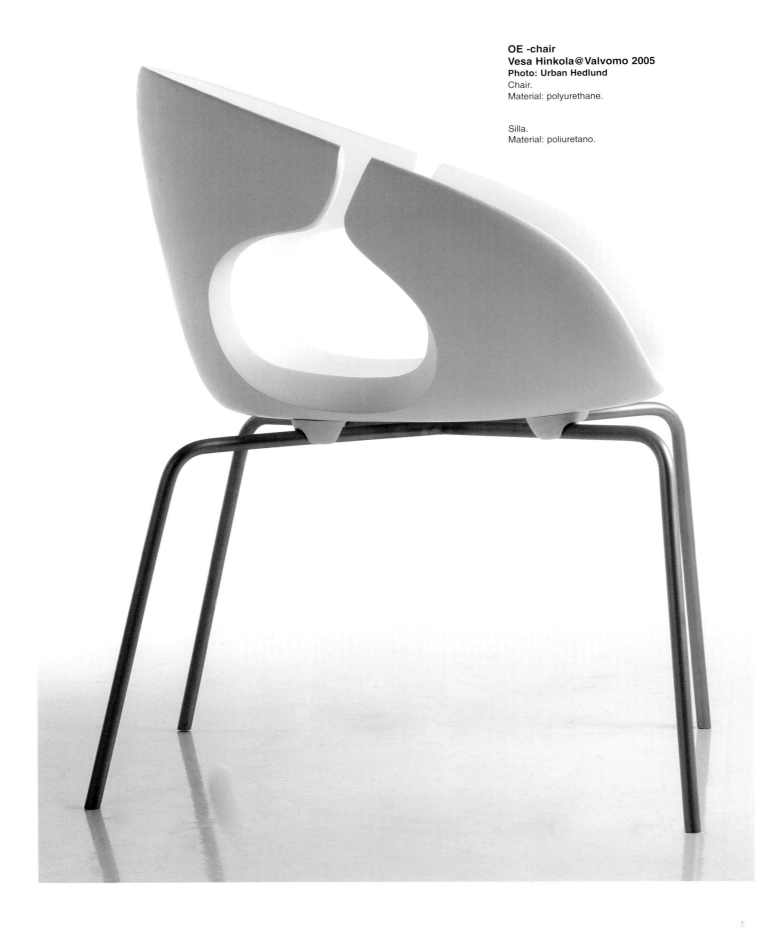

OE -chair
Vesa Hinkola@Valvomo 2005
Photo: Urban Hedlund
Chair.
Material: polyurethane.

Silla.
Material: poliuretano.

CHIP LOUNGER 1996
Teppo Asikainen, Ilkka Terho / Valvomo
Photo: Urban Hedlund
This chaise longue lies directly on the floor and can be
gently rocked thanks to its design and a piece of
polyurethane which cushions the movement.
Not currently available on the market.

Esta Chaise longue, se posa directamente en el suelo y
permite balancearse ligeramente gracias a su forma y a
una pieza de poliuretano que amortigua el movimiento.
De momento, no está disponible en el mercado.

THREESOME
Gudrun Lilja@Studiobility
3 Chairs or a bench?
Materials: silk, wood riddled with laser holes.

¿3 sillas o un banco?
Materiales: madera "silk printed" y cortada
por láser.

VISUAL INNER STRUCTURE
Gudrun Lilja@Studiobility
This designer, from a simple wooden chair
frame and a few threads of coloured wool has
given this chair a new lease of life.

A partir de la estructura de madera de una
silla, y de unos hilos de lana de color, esta
diseñadora ha dado una segunda vida a esta
silla

XXL Chair
Janneke Hooymans & Frank Tjepkema

To celebrate the company's one hundredth
anniversary, Arco asked 12 designers to propose what
they predict to be the future of furniture. The response
from the Tjep studio was this original design based on
our consumer society and the physical transformation
experienced by many people who become overweight.
The idea behind this chair suggests that the objects
around us can also be subjected to these
transformations.
A project carried out by Arco.

Para su centenario, Arco pidió a 12 diseñadores dar
su visión del futuro del mobiliario. La respuesta del
estudio Tjep ha sido esta original propuesta basándose
en la sociedad de consumo en la cual vivimos, y en el
cambio físico que sufren muchas personas con
sobrepeso.Esta silla plantea la posibilidad de que los
objetos que nos rodean también puedan sufrir de este
cambio de proporciones.
Proyecto realizado para Arco.

SMOKE 2002
Maarten Baas
Photo: Erwin Olaf

The entire Smoke collection is made from charred wood. The beauty and character of charred wood is captured within a hard wearing material, creating the strange sensation of being sat on charred wooden seats.

Materials: burnt furniture with epoxy coating.
Dimensions: 105cm x 72cm x 72cm
Produced and distributed by Moooi.
www.moooi.nl

Toda la colección Smoke está realizada con madera quemada. La belleza y el carácter de la madera quemada son capturados en un material duradero, creando la extraña sensación de sentarse en unas sillas quemadas.

Materiales: madera quemada con acabado epoxy.
Dimensiones: 105cm x 72cm x 72 cm
Producido y distribuido por Moooi.
www.moooi.nl

Table

METAL SIDE TABLE 2005
Ronan and Erwan Bouroullec
Photo: Paul tahon and Ronan Bouroullec
Small tables.
Materials: lacquered metal.
Produced by Vitra, Switzerland.
www.vitra.com

Mesitas.
Materiales: metal lacado.
Producido por Vitra, Suiza.
www.vitra.com

INSECT TABLE
Front design
Photo: Katja K
This original design is actually a reproduction of the tracks made by insects on the wood.

El original dibujo reproduce los conductos realizados por insectos en la madera.

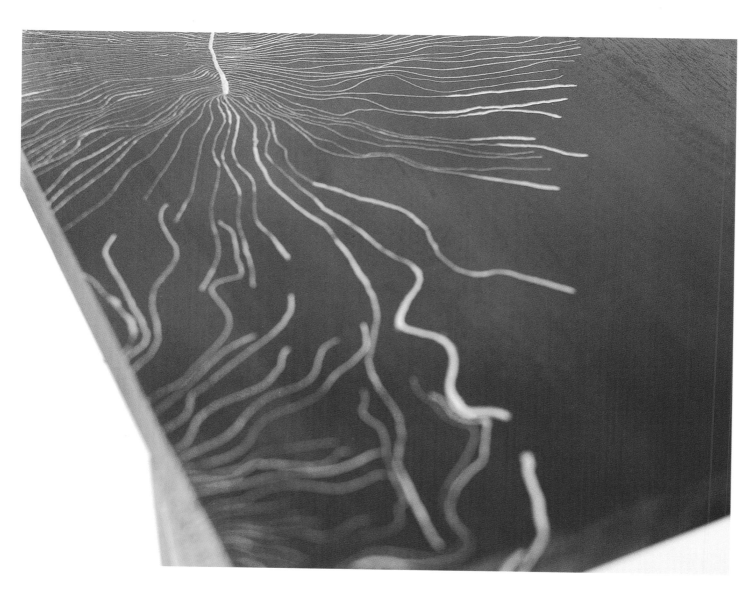

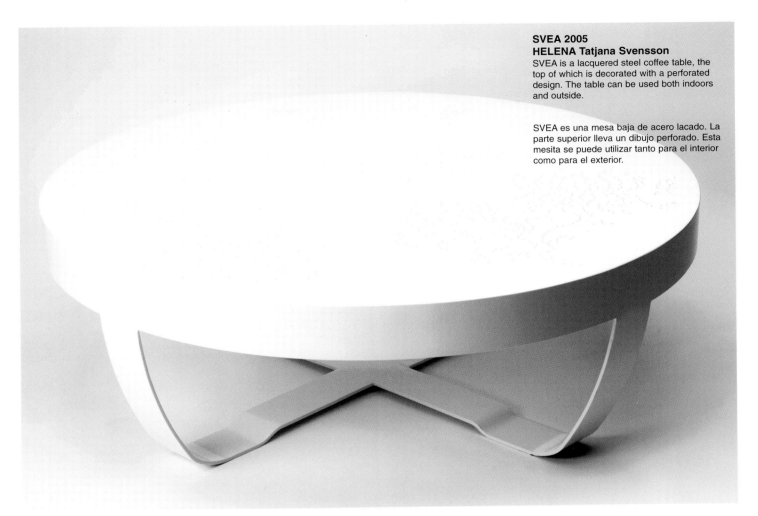

SVEA 2005
HELENA Tatjana Svensson

SVEA is a lacquered steel coffee table, the top of which is decorated with a perforated design. The table can be used both indoors and outside.

SVEA es una mesa baja de acero lacado. La parte superior lleva un dibujo perforado. Esta mesita se puede utilizar tanto para el interior como para el exterior.

TRETEAU
Big-Game
"Heritage in Progress"
Photo: Milo Keller

For those who have just moved in, these practical trestles are cheap, easy to assemble and perfect for adding a touch of classic "Chic" to the interiors. The design of this wooden chipboard piece pays a somewhat modernized form of homage to the "régence" style.
Materials: Wooden chipboard sheets.
Dimensions: 70cm x 25cm x H75cm
Pruduced by Ligne Roset.

Para los que se acaban de instalar, estos funcionales caballetes, baratos y fáciles de llevar son perfectos para dar un toque "Chic" y clásico a su interior. El perfil de madera conglomerada de este objeto es un homenaje actualizado del estilo "régence".
Materiales: Láminas de madera aglomerada.
Dimensiones: 70cm x 25cm x H75cm
Producido por Ligne Roset.

MUTTON 2005
Barnaby Bradford
The secret of this table is concealed beneath the tablecloth. At first glance it appears to be old table but in reality it is a plain pine IKEA table fitted with old legs.
Dimensions: 75cm x 135cm x 74cm

Debajo de este mantel se esconde el secreto de esta mesa. A primera vista estamos viendo una mesa antigua. Se trata en realidad de una simple mesa de pino de IKEA con patas antiguas.
Dimensiones: 75 cm x 135 cm x 74 cm

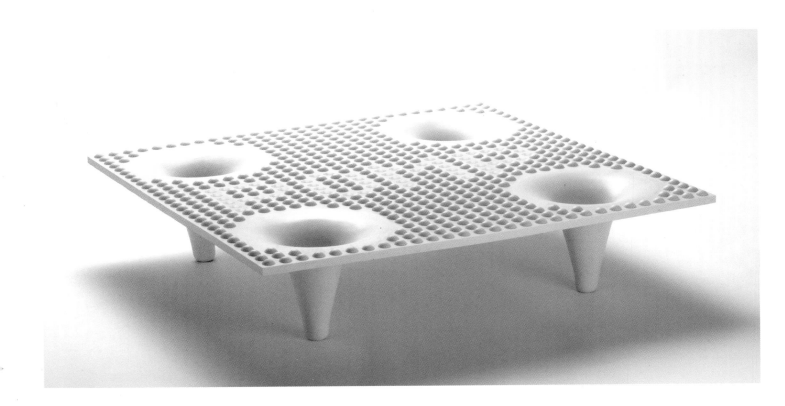

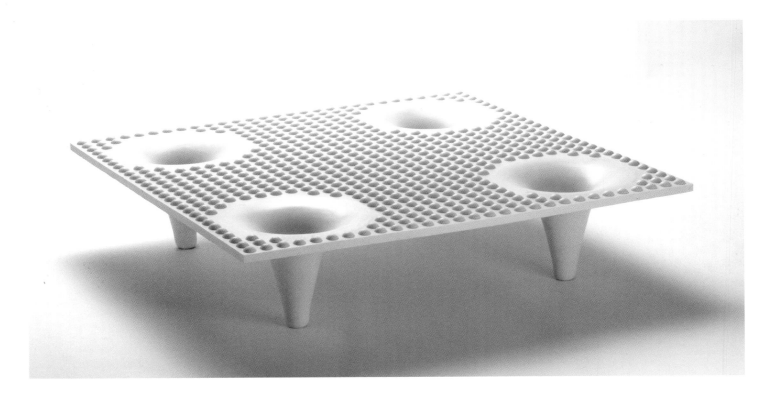

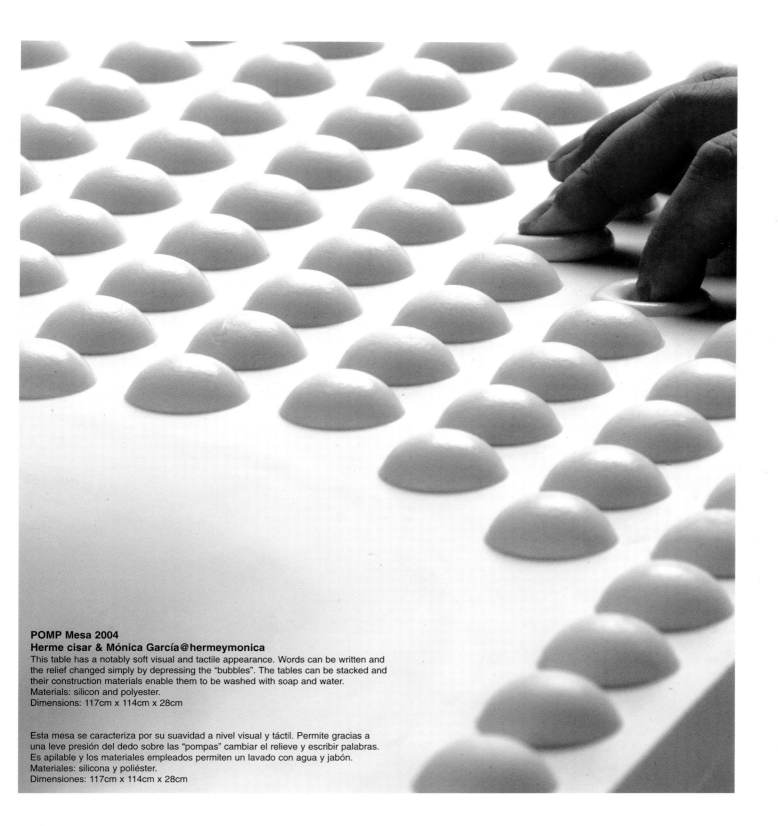

POMP Mesa 2004
Herme cisar & Mónica García@hermeymonica
This table has a notably soft visual and tactile appearance. Words can be written and
the relief changed simply by depressing the "bubbles". The tables can be stacked and
their construction materials enable them to be washed with soap and water.
Materials: silicon and polyester.
Dimensions: 117cm x 114cm x 28cm

Esta mesa se caracteriza por su suavidad a nivel visual y táctil. Permite gracias a
una leve presión del dedo sobre las "pompas" cambiar el relieve y escribir palabras.
Es apilable y los materiales empleados permiten un lavado con agua y jabón.
Materiales: silicona y poliéster.
Dimensiones: 117cm x 114cm x 28cm

SNOW
Nendo@swedese

Coffee table.
Materials: Tempered safety glass,
white lacquered chipboard.
Dimensions:
70cm x 70cm, Height 29.5
125cm x 70cm, Height 29.5
Made by Swedese.
www.swedese.com

Mesita de salón.
Materiales: Cristal de seguridad
templado, Madera aglomerada
lacada blanca.
Dimensiones:
70cm x 70cm, Altura 29,5
125cm x 70cm, Altura 29,5
Fabricado por Swedese.
www.swedese.com

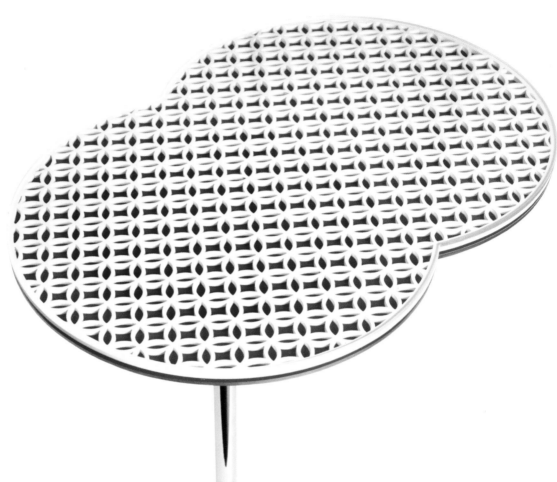

MOTIF Table system
Joe Doucet@intotonyc
This table is born from the relationship between a mass of circles. The decorative pattern is created by two circles joined together by their radii. Available in a range of heights and with different decorative designs from the most minimalist to the most baroque, but always related to circles.
Materials: acrylic, polycarbonate and polished stainless steel.

Esta mesa nace de la relación de una multitud círculos. El motivo es el encuentro de dos círculos en sus radios.Está disponibe en varias alturas, y con varios motivos, desde el más minimalista hasta el más barroco, pero eso sí, siempre relacionado con el círculo.
Materiales: acrílico, policarbonato y acero inoxidable pulido.

Dimensions / Dimensiones:
Side   45cm x 61cm x 40,5cm
Table 75cm x 61cm x 40,5cm
Bar   100cm x 61cm x 40,5cm

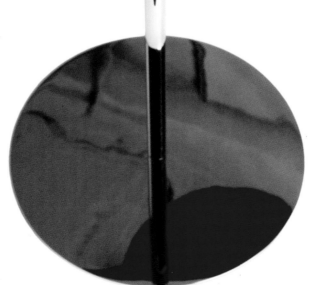

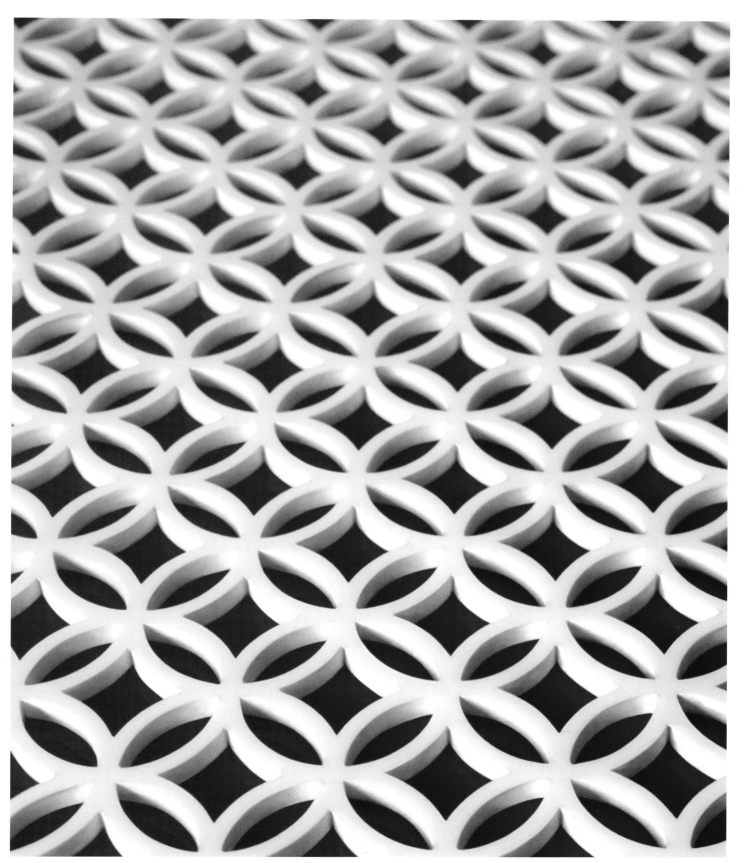

NEW ANTIQUES 2005
Marcel Wanders

This set of tables, chairs, and seats are made from turned wood with a black lacquer finish. The chair bottoms (with or without arms) are all filled with polyurethane foam and covered in either plain or textured black leather. A back support cushion is available for the twin seat made from the same leather.
The table tops are in smoked glass.

Dimensions:
Chair: 47cm x 48cm x78cm
Armchair: 57cm x 48cm x78cm
Twin seat: 73cm x 74cm x60cm
High table: ø 35cm x 50cm
Low table: ø 60cm x 38cm
Made by Cappellini.
www.cappellini.it

Esta serie de mesas sillas y sillón está realizada en madera torneada lacada negra. La silla (con o sin brazo) y el sillón tienen el asiento relleno de espuma de poliuretano y forrado de piel negra lisa o trabajada. Un cojín de respaldo del mismo cuero del asiento está disponible para el sillón.El tablero de las mesas está realizado con cristal ahumado.

Dimensiones:
silla: 47cm x 48cm x78cm
Silla con brazos: 57cm x 48cm x78cm
Sillón: 73cm x 74cm x60cm
Mesa alta: ø 35cm x 50cm
Mesa baja: ø 60cm x 38cm
Fabricado por Cappellini.
www.cappellini.it

DESIGN BY MECHANICS.
Front design

At first it trembles a little, learns to walk a few days later and is finally able to move for itself. The table, a new quadruped?

Tiembla un poco al principio, aprende a caminar pocos dias despues para, por fin, moverse por sí misma.
La mesa, ¿un nuevo cuadrúpedo?

ET tables
Reynold Rodriguez

A bedside table with an integrated magazine rack.
Materials: Polyester resin and fibreglass.
Dimensions: 56cm x 56cm x 46cm

Mesita de noche con revistero integrado.
Materiales: Resina de poliéster y fibra de cristal.
Dimensiones: 56cm x 56cm x 46cm

INNER BEAUTY
Gudrun Lilja

Every piece of furniture in this range is completely
unique. Made from laser cut wood veneer assembled
at random, creating an original design every time.
The cutting technique leaves the surface of the wood
in its natural shade, whilst the edges are darkened
by the heat generated in the cutting process. These
pieces of furniture can be used either as coffee
tables, benches or stools.

Cada pieza de esta serie de muebles es única.
Realizadas en madera contra-chapada
cortada por láser y montadas al azar, hace que el
motivo final sea diferente. La técnica de corte
utilizada deja la superficie de la plancha de madera
de color natural, mientras los lomos adquieren un
color oscuro debido a la quemadura generada
durante el corte. Se pueden utilizar como mesitas,
bancos o taburetes.

Shelving

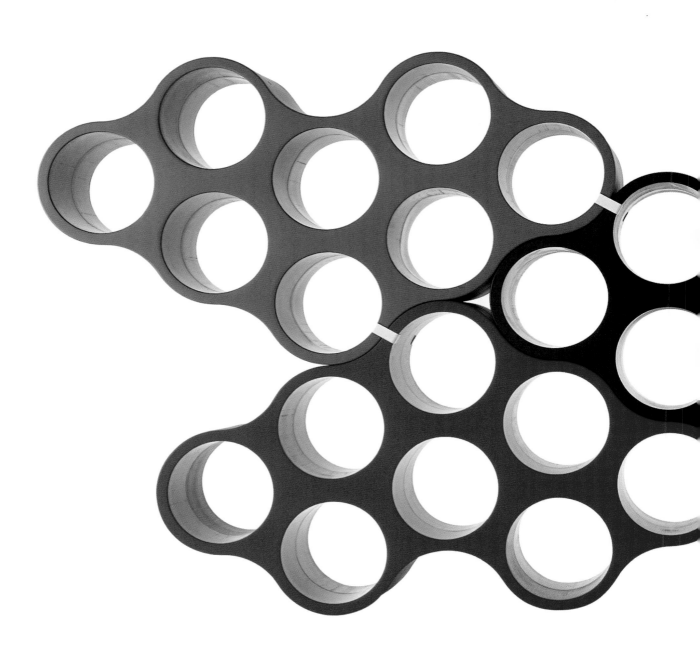

CLOUD 2004
Erwan and Ronan Bouroullec
Modular stacking bookcase.
Initially in white only, now available in various colours:
red, light green and dark green.
Also available with backlighting.
Material: polypropylene.
Dimensions: 187.5cm x 45cm x 105cm
Made by Cappellini.
www.cappellini.it

Biblioteca modular monobloque.
Inicialmente creada en color blanco, está ahora disponible en varios colores:
rojo, verde claro y verde oscuro.
También disponible con iluminación interna.

Materiales: polipropileno.
Dimensiones: 187,5cm x 45cm x 105cm
Fabricado por Cappellini.
www.cappellini.it

Photo: Ronan Bouroullec

OBLIQUE 2002
Marcel Wanders
Photo: Maarten van Houten

This original bookcase allows magazines and books to be displayed decoratively, simply and without having to make holes in the walls. A combination of simplicity and beauty.

Materials: MDF
Colours: white / black / red/ orange
Dimensions:
210cm x 105cm x 6cm
286cm x 105cm x 6cm
Produced and distributed by Moooi.

Esta original estantería permite presentar revistas y libros de forma decorativa, sencillísima y sin agujerear la pared. Sencillez y belleza.

Materiales: MDF
Colores: Blanco / negro / rojo / naranja
Dimensiones:
210cm x 105cm x 6 cm
286cm x 105cm x 6 cm
Producido y distribuido por Moooi.

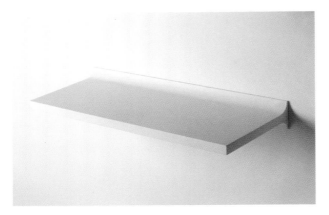

MOULURES UTILES 2003
Mathieu Lehanneur

Useful mouldings.
Shelves, a CD unit, and a bench.
Modular pieces made from synthetic plaster cast to be fixed to the wall. These mouldings are designed to blend in with the architecture. The furniture is integrated into the walls and blends into the surroundings. The mouldings, formerly used for ornamentation and a blatant outdoor display of ostentatious wealth have been duly transformed into an indoor display of comfort.
Materiales: Resin filled plaster cast.
Editor: FR66, Paris.
Made by Atelier Sédap, France
Technical advice: Bruno Tainturier.

Molduras útiles.
Estanterías, módulo para CD y banco.
Elementos modulares en yeso sintético a fijar en la pared. Éstas molduras, están pensadas para fusionar el mobiliario con la obra arquitectónica. Los muebles se integran en las paredes, y desaparecen del entorno. Las molduras eran antiguamente utilizadas como ornamento y como señal exterior de riqueza ostentosa. Éstas se han convertido en señal interior de confort.
Materiales: Yeso cargado con resina.
Editor: FR66, París.
Fabricado por Atelier Sédap, Francia.
Consejo técnico: Bruno tainturier.

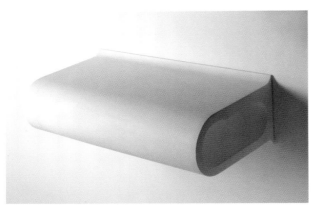

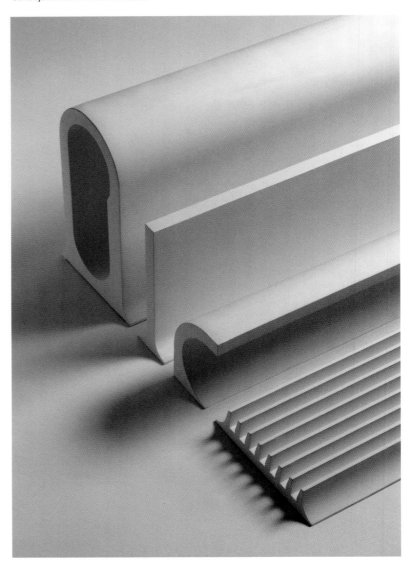

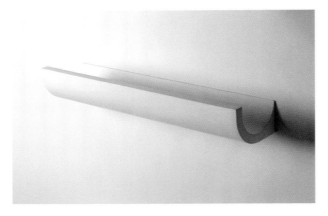

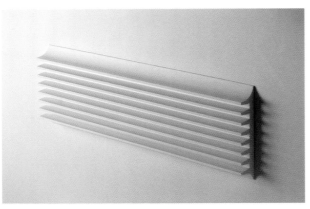

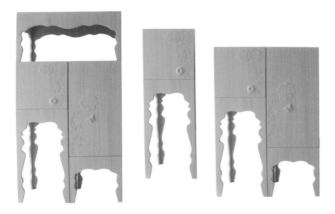

FLAT PACK ANTIQUES
Gundrun Lilja

This self assembly, IKEA type, flat pack furniture collection is the perfect example of a modern reinterpretation of antique carved wooden furniture.
Each unit can be used either individually or combined to fill an entire wall.
For the nostalgic amongst us, these furniture units are an easy self assembly alternative.

Esta serie de muebles es el ejemplo perfecto de reinterpretación moderna de muebles antiguos de talla de madera, en un concepto de muebles a montar, empaquetados de forma plana a la manera de IKEA.
Pueden ser utilizados solos o combinados, llenando una pared entera.
Para los nostálgicos, estos muebles son una alternativa fácil de llevar y montar en casa.

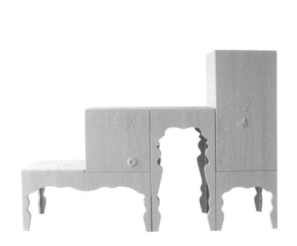

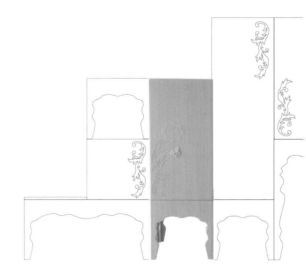

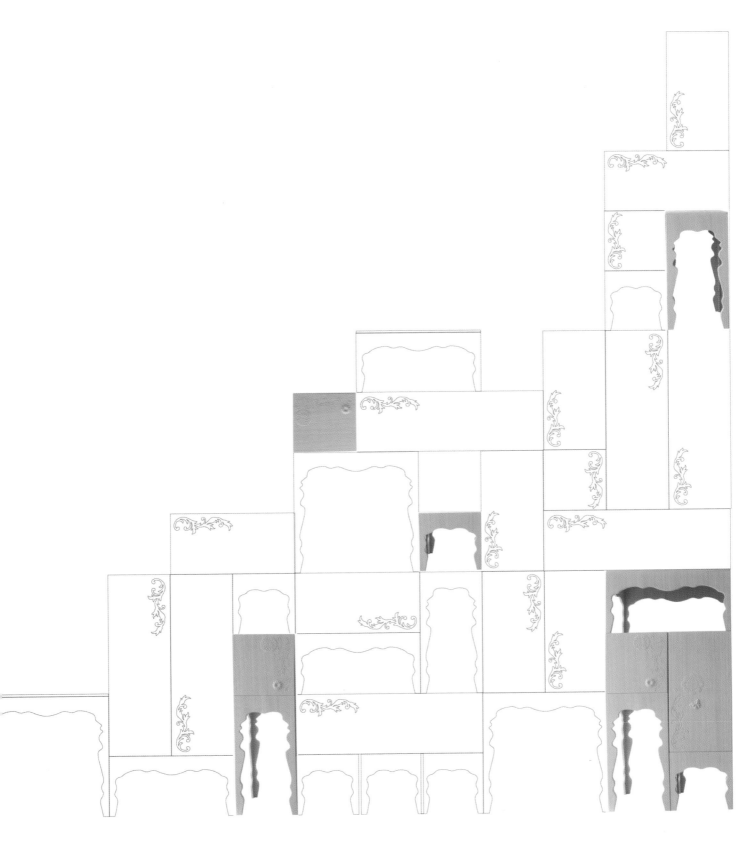

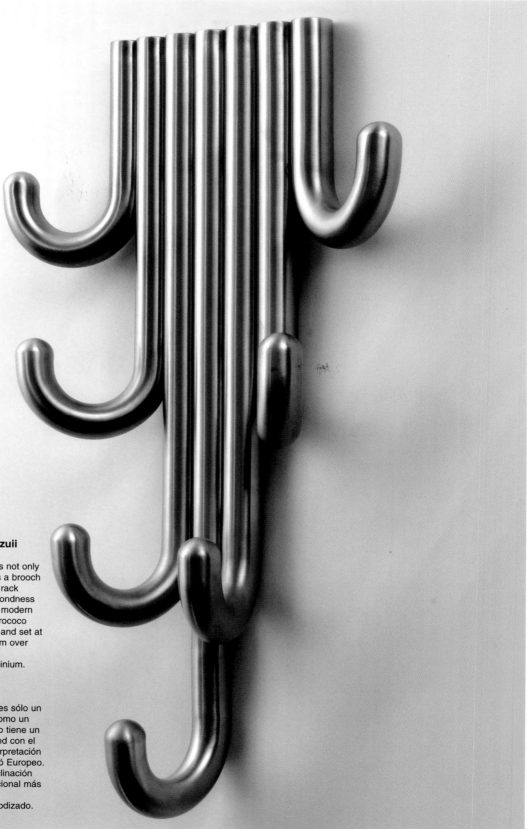

Wall Brooch 2005
Marcel Sigel & Alana Di Giacomo@zuii
Coat rack.
As its name would suggest, this coat rack is not only
a practical item but also decorative. Just as a brooch
adorns clothing, this highly decorative coat rack
should be hung on the wall with the same fondness
as a picture. The rack itself is a formal and modern
reinterpretation of the European baroque / rococo
style, with 7 hooks, each of a different size and set at
a different angle, making this a practical item over
and above its highly decorative value.
Materials: stainless steel or anodized aluminium.
Dimensions: 650mm 400cmm

Perchero de pared.
Como su nombre indica, este perchero no es sólo un
objeto práctico, sino también decorativo. Como un
broche lo haría sobre la ropa, este perchero tiene un
alto valor decorativo, y se cuelga en la pared con el
mismo cariño que un cuadro. Es una reinterpretación
formal y moderna del estilo barroco / rococó Europeo.
Sus 7 ganchos de diferentes tamaños e inclinación
hacen de este perchero un objeto muy funcional más
allá del alto valor decorativo.
Materiales: acero inoxidable o aluminio anodizado.
Dimensiones: 650mm 400cmm

WARDROBE
Front design

Y - coat rack 2002
Rane Vaskivuori@Valvomo
Coat rack / Perchero.
Made by / Fabricado por:
Idée Sputnik, Japan.
www.idee-online.com

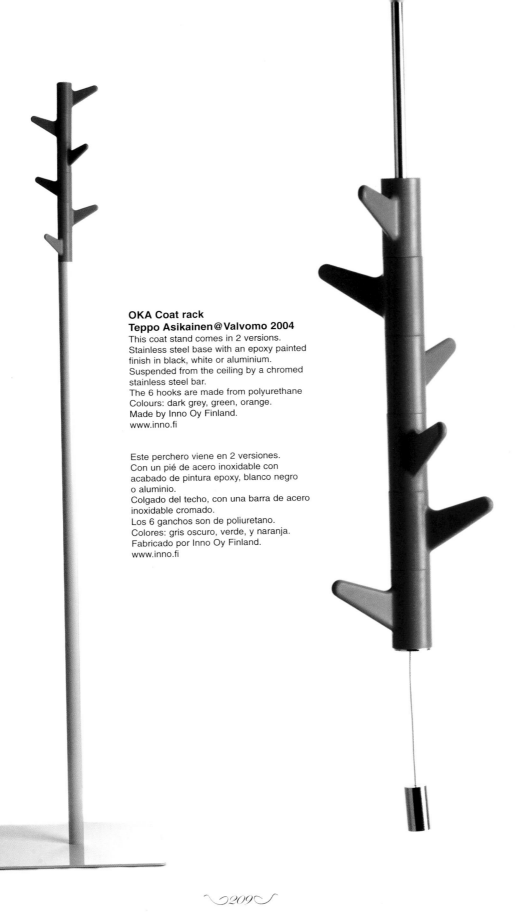

OKA Coat rack
Teppo Asikainen@Valvomo 2004
This coat stand comes in 2 versions.
Stainless steel base with an epoxy painted
finish in black, white or aluminium.
Suspended from the ceiling by a chromed
stainless steel bar.
The 6 hooks are made from polyurethane
Colours: dark grey, green, orange.
Made by Inno Oy Finland.
www.inno.fi

Este perchero viene en 2 versiones.
Con un pié de acero inoxidable con
acabado de pintura epoxy, blanco negro
o aluminio.
Colgado del techo, con una barra de acero
inoxidable cromado.
Los 6 ganchos son de poliuretano.
Colores: gris oscuro, verde, y naranja.
Fabricado por Inno Oy Finland.
www.inno.fi

Reflexion and Light

Mirror 2003
Ronan and Erwan Bouroullec
Photo: Paul Tahon
Mirror.
Materials: polished silver.
Dimensions: 30cm x 40cm x 8cm
Made by De Vecchi, Italy.
www.devecchi.com

Espejo.
Materiales: p pulida.
Dimensiones: 30cm x 40cm x 8cm
Fabricado por De Vecchi, Italy.
www.devecchi.com

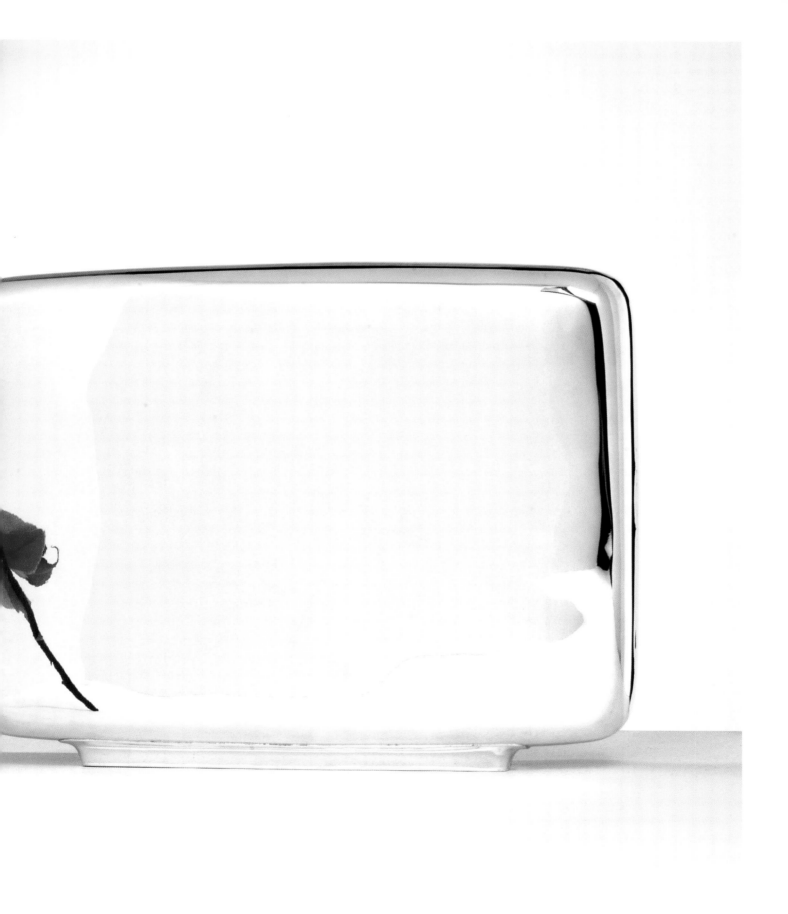

THE BATHROOM by Jaime Hayon

The Jaime Hayon collection is the first of a complete range of bathroom furniture which ArtQuitect Edition will be expanding as time goes on. Available items include everything from the most basic sink with the innovative and practical feature of being able to incorporate a range of accessories, up to the most elaborate combinations which lack for nothing.

Available finished in gold, platinum, yellow, black or white. The tables are optional and can be requested with or without an inbuilt towel rail, to be used more as a piece of house furniture if so desired. This flexibility is also carried through to the lamps, specifically designed for an environment in which there is water, but which can equally be used to light a passage or bedside table, as is the case with the mirrors with their spectacular shiny stainless steel surfaces, cut with the latest laser technology and a perfect representation of Hayon's reinterpretation of classic design.

La colección de Jaime Hayon es el inicio de un completo programa de mobiliario de baño que ArtQuitect Edition irá ampliando con el tiempo. Su oferta va desde el lavabo más básico, que aporta la novedad formal y funcional de poder incorporar diversos accesorios, hasta las composiciones más completas en las que no falta ningún detalle. En acabados de oro, platino y de colores amarillo, negro o blanco. Las mesas son opcionales y se pueden pedir con el toallero incorporado o no, para que si se quiere puedan utilizarse como un mueble más de la casa. Esa flexibilidad se traslada también a las lámparas, expresamente diseñadas para un entorno donde hay agua pero que igualmente pueden iluminar el pasillo o la mesita de noche, y a los espejos, donde brilla espectacularmente el de acero inoxidable cortado con la moderna tecnología del láser, que sintetiza a la perfección el estilo de Hayon cuando reinterpreta las formas clásicas.

ArtQuitect Edition.

Espejo 2005
Jaime Hayon
Lasercut pulished stainless steel mirror.

Espejo de acero inoxidable cortado a láser.

Artquitect Edition.
www.artquitect.net

BATHROOM FURNITURE
Jaime Hayon

Sink.
Table without towel rail.
Mirror.
A return to those elegant bathrooms of bygone times which represented social status both at home and in the restaurant. A return to the past which looks to the future to bring these beautiful objects back into our present day lives. The luxury of fine workmanship, democratized by modern yet traditional production methods, in this case from the very same company which created this elegance in the past. The lacquered woods, the crystalline ceramic and the precious metal finishes are updated versions of gold silver.
Chic and sophisticated. Brilliant in terms of both conception and production. Hayon, inspired by the quality and aesthetics of bygone times has used today's technology and know how to recreate these slim elegant designs and baroque silhouettes.

Lavabo.
Mesa sin toallero.
Espejo.
La vuelta a los baños elegantes, como los de antaño, cuando eran espacios que representaban el estatus social en la casa o en el restaurante. Un retorno al pasado mirando al futuro. Para recuperar en nuestro tiempo la prestancia de los objetos bellos.El lujo de las cosas bien hechas. Democratizado por la moderna producción artesanal. Realizada por los mismos fabricantes que creaban la elegancia en el pasado. Las maderas lacadas, la cerámica cristalina y los acabados de metal precioso que ponen al día los dorados y plateados de siempre.

Chic y sofisticado. Brillante en su concepción y también en la realización. Hayon se inspira en la calidad de los materiales y en la estética de otro tiempo, en las formas estilizadas y las siluetas barrocas, pero usa la tecnología de hoy para desarrollarlas y pone el ingenio para recrearlas.

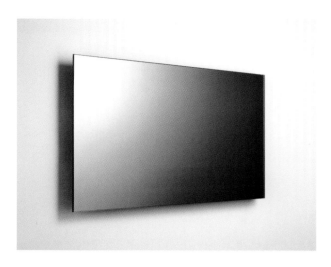

LED Mirror
Suck UK
Mirror with LED screen.
Directly connected to a PC, it is possible to display the date, time and predetermined messages of up to 4000 characters in different fonts together with special effects.
Dimensions: 65cm x 40cm.

Espejo con sistema LED.
Puede aparecer la fecha, la hora, y mensajes personalizados predeterminados de hasta 4000 caracteres, con efectos y diferentes fuentes, gracias a una conexión con un PC..
Dimensiones: 65cm x 40cm.

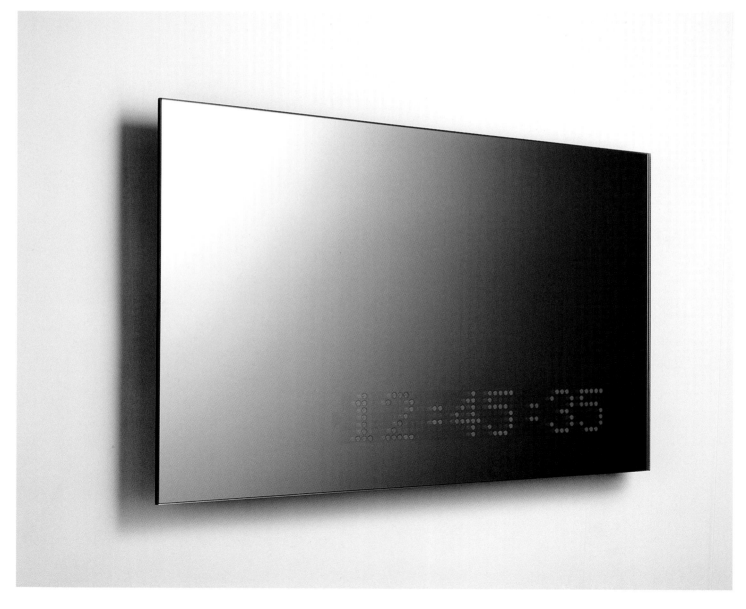

NEON MIRROR
Suck UK

Available in two versions, baroque or stainless steel and it is possible to choose the text or design of the neon installed behind the mirror.
The neon light is no longer visible when switched off.

Disponible en dos versiones, barroco o de acero inoxidable, es posible elegir el texto o el dibujo del neón que se encuentra detrás del espejo.
Una vez apagado el neón es invisible.

MIRROR PUZZLE 2003
Tobias Wong.
Mirror puzzle.
Espejo Puzzle.

MIRROIR GHOST 2001
Olivier Sidet
Photo : Olivier Sidet

A feature of this mirror is that it reflects the surroundings but not the image of the person looking into it.

Materials: mirror glass, optic coating and aluminium.
Limited edition of 30.
Tools Galerie, París 2001.

Este espejo tiene la característica de reflejar todo el entorno pero no deja a la persona que se mira, ver su propio reflejo.
Materiales : cristal espejo, capa óptica y aluminio.
Edición limitada a 30 ejemplares.
Tools Galerie, París 2001.

LOST 2003
Robert Stadler
Photo: Patrick Gries.
Mirror-fan.
Fan blades become transparent once in motion. Lost
uses reflective fan blades to create a moving mirror,
producing an almost transparent, phantasmagorical
reflected image which appears to be levitating.
Materials: acrylic mirror, electric motor.
Dimensions: Al 50 cm, ø 140 cm
Limited edition of 6 + 1 at KlausEngelhorn 22,
Vienna.

Las aspas de un ventilador una vez en rotación,
parecen ser transparentes. Lost juega con las aspas
reflectantes para obtener un espejo en movimiento,
creando una imagen que parece levitar. Aparece una
imagen fantasmagórica casi transparente.
Materiales: espejo acrílico, motor eléctrico.
Dimensiones: Al 50 cm, ø 140 cm
Edición limitada: 6 ej + 1ej KlausEngelhorn22,
Viena.

+336+ 2004
Robert Stadler
Photo: Patrick Gries.
Mirror.
+336+ is far more than a mirror. It can in fact
receive SMS messages from a mobile phone. The
messages are displayed on the mirror's surface as
illuminated moving text which appears whenever
anyone approaches.
Dimensions: 70cm x 55cm
Limited edition of 20 + 3 at Galerie Dominique Fiat,
Paris

Espejo.
+336+ es más que un espejo. Es capaz de recibir
un SMS mandado desde un teléfono móvil. Los
mensajes recibidos se leen directamente en la
superficie del espejo como un texto luminoso en
movimiento que aparece cuando alguien se acerca.
Dimensiones: 70 cm x 55 cm
Edición limitada: 20 ej + 3 ej Galerie Dominique
Fiat, París.

MIROIR POUR FONTAINE 2005
Nicolas Le Moigne
An original way to transform any fountain
into a bathroom. This object has been
specially designed for a forthcoming
exhibition in 2006. The idea was to create
an assortment of objects for the urban
environment. Once the exhibition is over,
the objects will be donated to the city of
Lausanne.

Exhibition: INOUT, Mudac, Lausanne,
Switzerland, 2006
Material: stainless steel mirror.
Dimensions: 30cm x 45cm x 10cm

Una manera original de convertir cualquier
fuente en un cuarto de baño. Este objeto
ha sido realizado especialmente para una
exposición prevista para el 2006. La idea
era crear un serie de objetos para el
entorno urbano. Una vez terminada la
exposición los objetos serán regalados a la
cuidad de Lausana.

Exposición: INOUT, Mudac, Lausana,
Suiza, 2006
Materiales: espejo de acero inoxidable.
Dimensiones: 30cm x 45cm x 10cm

LAMPE SOUPLE
Big Game
This silicon lamp has been inspired by and
changes the significance of the plastic cones
which initially covered the hole in ceilings and
surplus electric cable. Hanging ceiling lights also
predetermined the position of the dining suite
within the room. Big Game has nonetheless
turned this factor on its head making this lamp
an example of mobility.
Materials: silicon.
Dimensions: 10cm x 10cm x 10cm
Operates by colour interchangeable LED.

Esta lámpara de silicona se inspira y cambia el
sentido de los conos de plástico que inicialmente
tapan el agujero del techo y el sobrante de cable
eléctrico. Las lámparas colgando del techo
determinaban también la posición de la mesa y
de las sillas en la habitación. Pues Big Game
Invierte también esta característica haciendo de
esta lámpara un ejemplo de movilidad. ¡Doble
cambio de sentido!
Materiales: silicona.
Dimensiones: 10cm x 10cm x 10cm
Funciona con LED de color intercambiable.

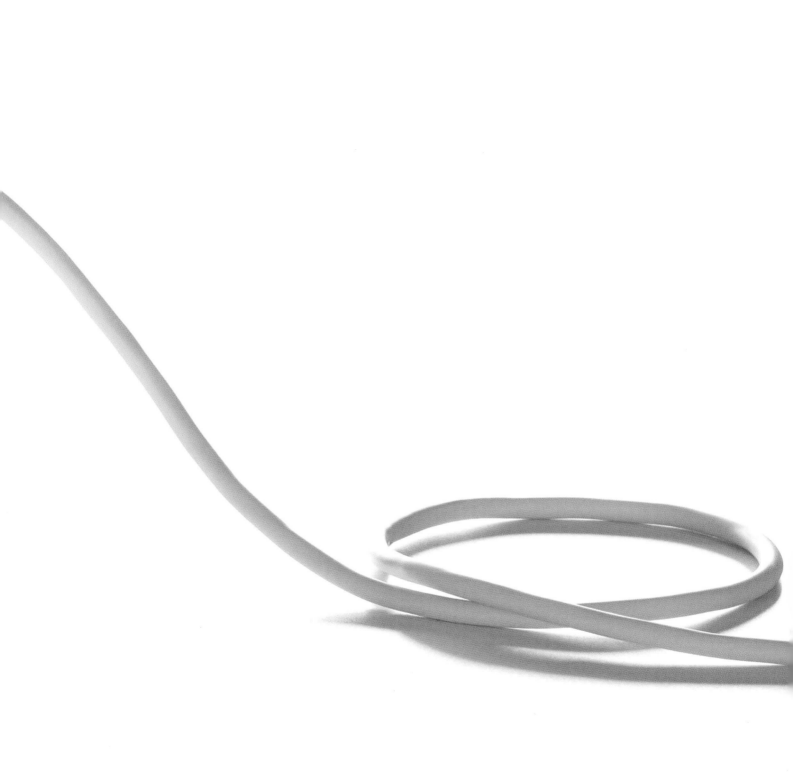

LIGHT WHITE
Jan Borchies

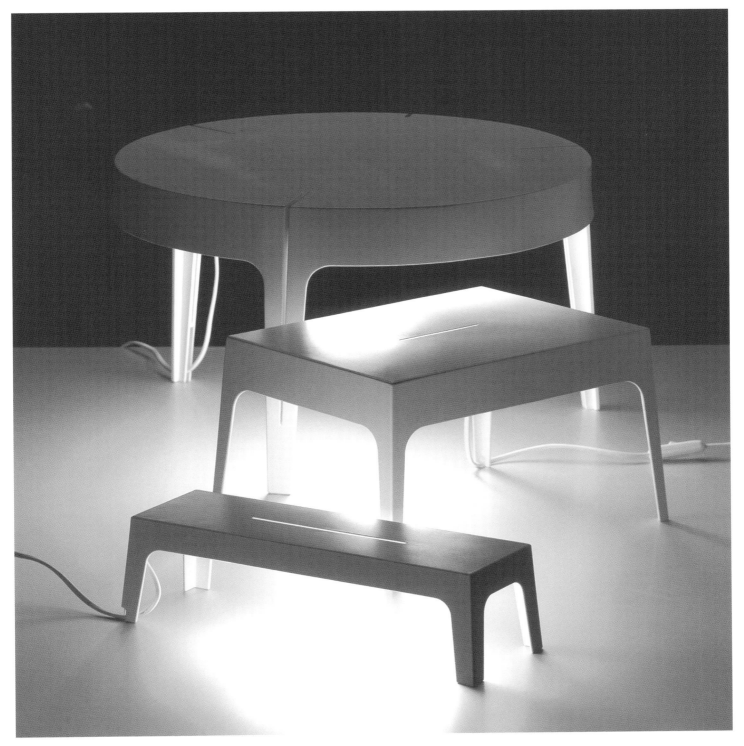

ZIA, ZIO, NIPOTINO 2003
Sebastian Bergne
Table light.
A range of plastic tables in different shapes and sizes with an integrated light providing any room with soft inviting illumination projected directly on to the floor.
Materials: ABS.
Produced by Luceplan.

Serie de mesitas de plástico de diferente tamaño y forma con luz integrada para iluminar de forma suave y acogedora un espacio proyectando la luz directamente en el suelo.
Materiales: ABS.
Producido por Luceplan.

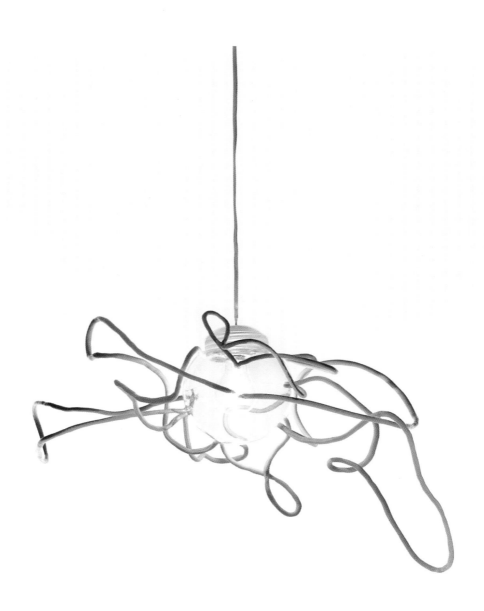

FLY LAMP
Front design
Photo Katja K
Imagine the frenzied movement of an
insect attracted by the light of a bulb.
Here it is fully materialized.

Imaginar el movimiento frenético de un
insecto atraído por la luz de una bombilla.
Pues aquí lo tenemos materializado.

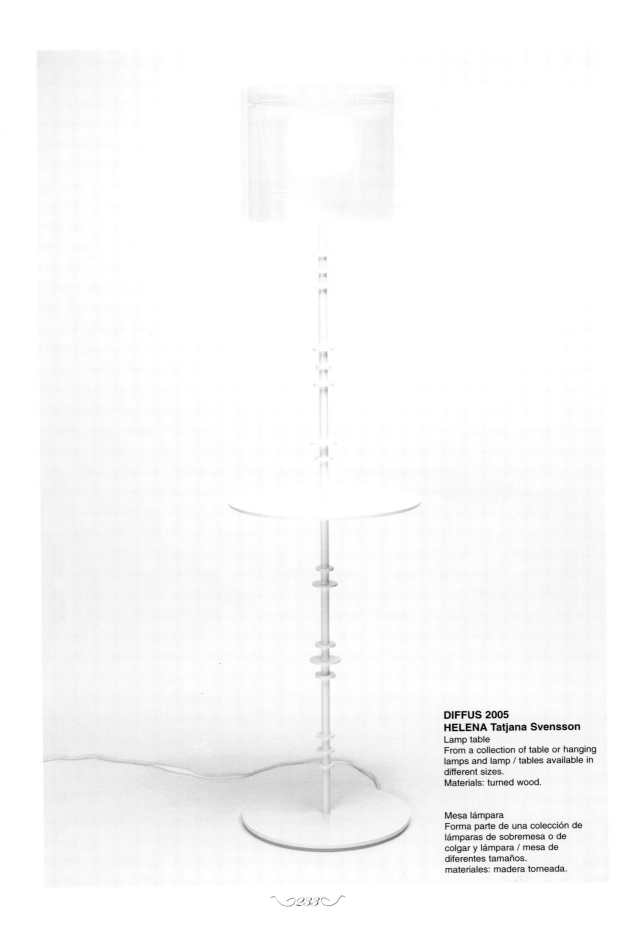

DIFFUS 2005
HELENA Tatjana Svensson
Lamp table
From a collection of table or hanging
lamps and lamp / tables available in
different sizes.
Materials: turned wood.

Mesa lámpara
Forma parte de una colección de
lámparas de sobremesa o de
colgar y lámpara / mesa de
diferentes tamaños.
materiales: madera torneada.

LIGHT IN TIME
Adrien Rovero, Augustin Scott de Martinville & Nicolas Le Moigne
Ecole cantonale d'art de Lausanne (ECAL)
Photo: ECAL

This joint project from the Swarovski workshop in collaboration with the famous "école cantonale d'art de Lausanne" (ECAL) (Switzerland), looks into possible new and original uses for the crystal. Light in time is one of these precious creations. Passing time is marked by the pendulum swinging in the halo of light produced on the wall. Both light and crystal are subtly linked to time. When the pendulum is still, it becomes reminiscent of the pull cord on a lamp and we are able to fully appreciate the crystal cutting. When the pendulum is moving, luminous arcs are reflected on the wall reminding us of the relation between time and motion.

Este proyecto ha surgido del workshop organizado por Swarovski en colaboración con la famosa "école cantonale d'art de Lausanne" (ECAL) (Suiza) para estudiar las posibilidades de utilización del cristal de forma nueva y original. Light in time es una de estas preciosas creaciones. El paso del tiempo está marcado por la oscilación del péndulo en el halo de luz formado en la pared. La luz y el cristal están siempre unidos al tiempo de una manera sutil. Cuando el péndulo está quieto, se convierte en una reminiscencia de una cuerda-interruptor de la lámpara y podemos apreciar las tallas en el cristal. Cuando el péndulo está en movimiento, se reflejan arcos luminosos en la pared que nos recuerdan la relación entre el tiempo y el movimiento.

LÁMPARA
Jaime Hayon
Materials: ceramic.
Dimensions: H 54cm
Made and distributed by ArtQuitect.
www.artquitect.net

Materiales: cerámica.
Dimensiones: H 54cm
Realizado y distribuido por ArtQuitect.
www.artquitect.net

DEAR INGO
Ron Gilad

This lamp is a hybrid between the classic candelabra and purely functional office lamps. The surprising result is a variety of lighting configurations produced by a somewhat unusual modern candelabra. Dimensions: 100cm x 80cm (ø x Al) Produced and distributed by Moooi. www.moooi.nl

Esta lámpara es una hibridación del candelabro clásico y de las funcionales lámparas de oficina. El resultado es sorprendente y ofrece varias configuraciones de luz para este peculiar candelabro moderno. Dimensiones: 100cm x 80cm (ø x Al) Producido y distribuido por Moooi. www.moooi.nl

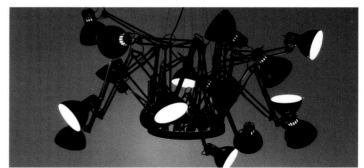

SMOKE CHANDELIER
Maarten Baas
Lamp / Chandelier.
Dimensions: 55cm x 65cm
Materials: chared wood with epoxy finish.
Produced and distributed by Moooi.
www.moooi.nl

Lámpara.
Dimensiones: 55cm x 65cm
Materiales: madera quemada con acabado
de epoxy.
Fabricado y distribuido por Moooi.
www.moooi.nl

UPLIGHT & DOWNLIGHT 2003

A bold step away from classic ceramic design can be found in UPLIGHT and DOWNLIGHT of the porcelain lighting series. It uses a traditional technique that exploits the translucency of this strikingly delicate material, but delivers it towards a more forward looking formal approach. In casting the forms of mass-produced industrial lamps

Material: porcelain white matt bisque.
Produced by Fredrikson Stallard.

Lejos de la formas clásicas de los objetos de porcelana, estas lámparas nacen de la mezcla de la sensibilidad del material empleado y de la modernidad de las formas de un objeto puramente industrial.El resultado es sorprendente y la porcelana se vuelve translúcida al encender la luz.

Material: porcelana beige mate.
Producido por Fredrikson Stallard.

Pure Designers

André Klauser
(England / Germany)
(Inglaterra / Alemania)

www.andreklauser.com
andre@andreklauser.com

65 - 66 Charlotte Road
London EC2A 3PE

Barnaby Bradford
(England)
(Inglaterra)

www.barnabybarford.co.uk
barnaby@thrink.net

23 Adeney Close
London W6 8ES UK

Big Game
(Suitzerland / Belgium)
(Suiza / Bélgica)

Grégoire Jeanmonod
Elric Petit
Augustin Scott de
Martinville

www.big-game.ch
contact@big-game.ch

Avelines, 6
1004 Lausanne
Suisa

1, rue d'Andenne
1060 Bruxelles
Bélgica

Foto: Milo Keller

Cédric Ragot
(France)
(Francia)

cedric.ragot@free.fr

54 rue Marceau
93100 Montreuil

chris kabel
(Netherlands)
(Paises Bajos)

mail@chriskabel.com
www.chriskabel.com

po box 21660
3001 ar Rotterdam

CuldeSac
(Spain)
(España)

Pilar Roger
Alberto Martínez
Pepe García
Francisco Pons

www.culdesac.es
culdesac @ culdesac . es

grabiel y gálan 9, bajo/dch
46017 Valencia

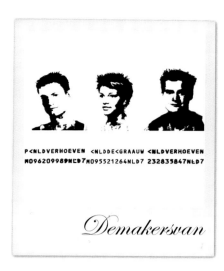

Demakersvan
(Netherlands)
(Países Bajos)
Jeroen Verhoeven
Judith de Graauw
Joep Verhoeven

www.demakersvan.com
contact@demakersvan.com

Marconistraat 52 Haven 357
3029 AK Rotterdam

Demakersvan

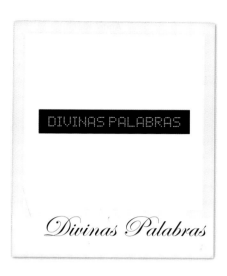

Divinas Palabras
(Spain)
(España)

Quique Baeza Director creativo
Ricard Giró Director ejecutivo

www.divinaspalabras.com
info@divinaspalabras.com

Rambla del Raval 2b 1/2
08001 Barcelona

Divinas Palabras

Ecole cantonale d'art de Lausanne/écal
Haute école d'art et de design (HES·SO)
University of art and design Lausanne

éc a l

Ecal

Ecole cantonale d'art de Lausanne (ECAL)
Pierre Keller Director
(Suitzerland)
(Suiza)

www.ecal.ch
pierre.keller@ecal.ch

4, avenue de l'Elysee
CH-1006 Lausanne

Frederic Ruyant
(France)
(Francia)

www.fredericruyant.com
frdesign@aol.com

7 rue de Beauce 75003
Paris

Frédéric Ruyant

Front design

Front design
(Sweden)
(Suecia)

Sofia Lagerkvist
Charlotte von der Lancken
Anna Lindgren
Katja Sävström

www.frontdesign.se
everyone@frontdesign.se

Tegelviksgatan 20
116 41 Stockholm

Greenfortune

Greenfortune
(Sweden)
(Suecia)

Hans Andersson
Johan Svensson

www.greenfortune.com
hans@greenfortune.com
johan@greenfortune.com

Gudrun Lilja

**Studio bility
(Iceland)
(Islandia)
Gudrun Lilja
John Asgeir**

www.bility.is
gl@bility.is
ja@bility.is

Bygggardar 10
170 Seltjarnarnes

Gudrun Lilja

**Guillaume delvigne
(France)
(Francia)**

www.guillaumedelvigne.com
guillaumedelvigne@hotmail.com

2, rue Tolain
75020 - Paris - France

Guillaume Delvigne

**Harry Allen & Associates
(USA)
(EEUU)**

patrick@harryallendesign.com
www.harryallendesign.com

207 Avenue A
New York, NY 10009

Harry Allen

**Helena Tatjana Svensson
(Sweden)
(Suecia)**

www.helenatatjana.com
info@helenatatjana.com

Burspråksvägen 3
121 47 Johanneshov

*Helena Tatjana
Svensson*

**Herme y Mónica
Herme Ciscar
Mónica García
(Spain)
(España)**

www.hermeymonica .com
info@hermeymonica .com

c/ millares 2-5
e-46007 Valencia

Herme y Monica

**Intotonyc
Joe Doucet
Janet Doucet
(USA)
(EEUU)**

www.intotonyc.com
Joe@intotonyc.com
Janet@intotonyc.com
info@intotonyc.com

10 Liberty street nº36g
New York 10005

Intotonyc

**ionna Vautrin
(France)
(Francia)**

ionnavautrin@hotmail.com
16 rue Pache
75011 Paris

Iona Vautrin

**Jaime Hayon
(Spain)
(España)**

www.hayonstudio.com
info@hayonstudio.com

CREATIVE BASE
HAYON STUDIO BCN
Muntaner 88 2.1A
08011 Barcelona

Jaime Hayon

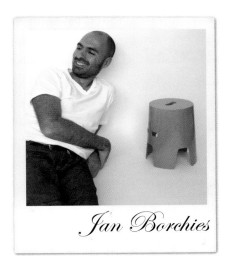

**Jan Borchies
(Sweden)
(Suecia)**

www.janborchies.com
info@janborchies.com

Terrängvägen 59, 129 48
Hägersten (Stockholm)

Jan Borchies

**Joris Laarman
(Netherlands)
(Países Bajos)**

www.jorislaarman.com
info@jorislaarman.com

Joris Laarman
Laan van Puntenburg 2
3035 ER Utrecht

Joris laarman

**Estudihac
Jose Manuel Ferrero
(Spain)
(España)**

www.estudihac.com
estudihac@estudihac.com

Jose manuel Ferrero

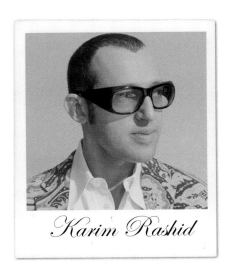

**Karim Rashid
(USA)
(EEUU)**

www.karimrashid.com
office@karimrashid.com

KARIM RASHID Inc.
357 West 17th St.
New-York. NY 10011

Karim Rashid

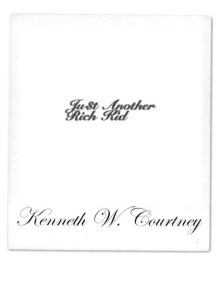

Kenneth W. Courtney
Ju$t Another Rich Kid
(USA)
(EEUU)

info@justanotherrichkid.com
www.justanotherrichkid.com

168 Second Avenue #305
New York, NY 10003

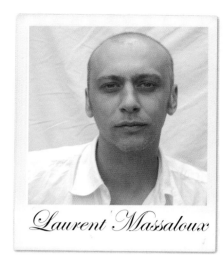

Laurent Massaloux
(France)
(Francia)

laurent@massaloux.net
www.massaloux.net

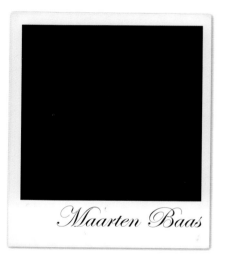

Maarten Baas
(Netherlands)
(Países Bajos)

www.maartenbaas.com
mail@maartenbaas.com

BAAS ontwerpen
Eindhovenseweg 104
5582 HW WAALRE

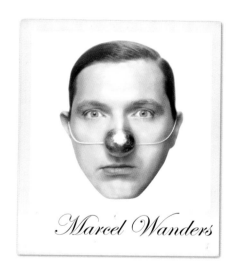

Marcel Wanders
(Netherlands)
(Países Bajos)

www.marcelwanders.com
femke@marcelwanders.com

Marcel Wanders Studio
Jacob Catskade 35
1052 BT Amsterdam

Mathieu Lehanneur
(France)
(Francia)

mlehanneur@clubinternet.fr

9-11 rue du Roule
75001 Paris

Meric Kara
(Turkey)
(Turquía)

www.merickara.com
meric@merickara.com

**Mixko
Nahoko Koyama
Alexander Garnett
(Japan / England)
(Japón / Inglaterra)**

www.mixko.net
nahoko@mixko.net
alex@mixko.net

MUJI

www.muji.com
press@muji.co.uk

Muji(UK) Press Office
41 Carnaby Street
London
W1F 7DX
UK

**Nendo inc.
(Japan)
(Japón)**

www.nendo.com
info@nendo.jp

4-1-20-2A Mejiro Toshima-ku
Tokyo 171-0031 Japan

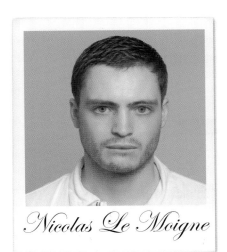

**Nicolas Le Moigne
(France / Suitzerland)
(Francia / Suiza)**

www.nicolaslemoigne.com
nicolas_lm@hotmail.com

3, Rue de la Tour
CH - 1004 Lausanne
Suiza

**Olivier Sidet
(France)
(Francia)**

www.oliviersidet.com
design@oliviersidet.com

**RADI DESIGNERS
(France)
(Francia)**

www.radidesigners.com
info@radidesigners.com

89, rue de Turenne
75003 Paris

**Rehti
(Finland)
(Finlandia)**

www.rehti.org
info@rehti.org

Mechelininkatu 16
FIN-00100 Helsinki

Aleksi Penttilä
www.aleksipenttila.com

Jari-Petri Voutilainen
www.jpvoutilainen.com

Mika Tolvanen
www.mikatolvanen.com

Mikko Laakkonen
www.mikkolaakkonen.com

**Reynold Rodriguez
(Puerto Rico)**

www.reynoldrodriguez.com
Contact@reynoldrodriguez.com

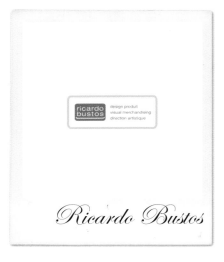

**Ricardo Bustos
(France)
(Francia)**

www.ricardobustos.com
ricijb@wanadoo.fr

57 Rue Charlot
75003 Paris

**Robert Stadler
(France)
(Francia)**

www.robertstadler.net
info@robertstadler.net

4 rue de Bretagne
75003 Paris

**Designfenzider
Ron Gilad
(USA)
(EEUU)**

www.designfenzider.com
info@designfenzider.com

93 Reade Street, Ste. 3
New York, NY 10013

**Ronan y Erwan Bouroullec
(France)
(Francia)**

www.bouroullec.com
info@bouroullec.com

23 rue du Buisson Saint-Louis
75 010 Paris

Rosaria Rattin
Kose Milano
(Italy)
(Italia)

Corso San Gottardo,22
20136 Milano

www.kosemilano.com
info@kosemilano.com

Rosaria Rattin

Sam Baron
(France / Portugal)
(Francia / Portugal)

sambaron@clix.pt

c/o Carinne Damon 21, rue
d'arcole 75004 Paris

rua fernandes tomás, 63, 4°,
1200-178 Lisboa

Sam Baron

Sebastian Bergne
(England / Italy)
(Inglaterra / Italia)

www.sebastianbergne.com
mail@sebastianbergne.com

Sebastian Bergne Ltd,
Design Office
2 Ingate Place
London SW8 3NS

Via Castiglione 90
40124 Bologna

Sebastian Bergne

SUCK UK LTD
(England)
(Inglaterra)
Designers and managing
directors
Sam & Jude

www.suck.uk.com
gemma@suck.uk.com

31 Regent Studios, Andrews
Rd, London E8 4QN

Suck Uk

Tany Aguiñiga
(USA)
(EEUU)

tanya@aguinigadesign.com
www.aguinigadesign.com

941 N. Vendome Street
Los Angeles, CA 90026
619-892-1506

Tanya Aguiñiga

Tjep
Frank Tjepkema
Janneke Hooymans
(Netherlands)
(Paises Bajos)

www.tjep.com
Frank Tjepkem

Weesperzijde 80B
1091 EJ Amsterdam

Tjep

Tobias Wong
(USA)
(EEUU)

www.brokenoff.com
tobias@brokenoff.com

Tobias Wong

Sakai Design Associate Co.
(Japan)
(Japón)
Representative director
Toshihiro Sakai

www.sakaidesign.com
info@sakaidesign.com

150-0001
6-25-8 '701' Jingumae
Shibuya
Tokyo

Toshihiko Sakai

Valeria Miglioli
(England / Italy)
(Inglaterra / Italia)

vallymiglioli@hotmail.com

Valeria Miglioli

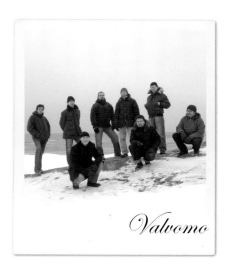

Valvomo Architects
(Finland)
(Finlandia)

www.valvomo.com
info@valvomo.com

Perämiehenkatu 12 E
FIN-00150 Helsinki
Finland

Valvomo

Zuii
Marcel Sigel
Alana Di Giacomo
(Australia)

www.zuii.com
info@zuii.com

GPO Box 5156
Melbourne, Victoria
Australia, 3001

Zuii

Fredrikson Stallard
(England)
(Inglaterra)

www.fredriksonstallard.com
info@fredriksonstallard.com

2 Glebe Road
London E8 4BD
UK

Fredrikson Stallard

Thanks, Gracias...

With thanks to all the selected designers and their press officers, and thanks also to the manufacturing companies and art galleries for their collaboration and assistance. To Louis for his professional advice.

Gracias a todos los diseñadores seleccionados, sus encargados de prensa, las empresas fabricantes y galerías de arte por su colaboración y ayuda. A Louis por sus consejos profesionales.

Pure design